每天10分钟
从零开始学
英语口语
提高篇

李琦◎编著

中国纺织出版社有限公司

图书在版编目（CIP）数据

每天10分钟：从零开始学英语口语. 提高篇 / 李琦 编著. -- 北京：中国纺织出版社有限公司，2022.8

ISBN 978-7-5180-8971-0

Ⅰ.①每… Ⅱ.①李… Ⅲ.①英语－口语－自学参考 资料 Ⅳ.①H319.9

中国版本图书馆CIP数据核字（2021）第203737号

责任编辑：武洋洋　　责任校对：高　涵　　责任印制：储志伟

中国纺织出版社有限公司出版发行

地址：北京市朝阳区百子湾东里A407号楼　邮政编码：100124

销售电话：010—67004422　传真：010—87155801

http://www. c-textilep. com

中国纺织出版社天猫旗舰店

官方微博 http://weibo. com/2119887771

三河市延风印装有限公司印刷　各地新华书店经销

2022年8月第1版第1次印刷

开本：880×1230　1 / 32　印张：6.5

字数：200千字　定价：45.00元

前 言
FOREWORD

有人说金字塔的魅力就在于它完美的建筑结构，有坚实深厚的基础，才造就了塔尖的辉煌。学好英文也是同样的道理，坚实的语言基础很多时候来源于大量的输入，量变达到质变，这种语言便能脱口而出，"语感"则应运而生。

《每天10分钟：从零开始学英语口语》系列图书共3册，分为入门篇、基础篇和提高篇。通过循序渐进的学习，让你练就纯熟地道的英语口语。

本书为《每天10分钟：从零开始学英语口语（提高篇）》，围绕与现代生活息息相关的话题，分为14个单元，每个单元按照学习难度分为"Basic初级基础""Intermediate 中级进阶""Advanced 高级飞跃"三个等级，每个等级内设置了"万用表达一览""万用表达详解""实用对话场景""跨文化交际小常识"四个板块，读者每天只需10分钟，即可掌握每个section的口语内容，学习最地道的表达句型和短语，同时还能了解西方国家的交际常识，避免交际中的尴尬。

本书是一本实用、有趣的英语口语用书，适用于英语学习者自学，或是查阅相关话题的表达，也可以作为教学机构的英语口语参考用书。相信读者通过对本书的学习，能够达到举一反三、脱口而出、随心所欲说英语的水平。

编著者

2022年7月

目　录

CONTENTS

Unit 1

Body Language I
身体语言（一）

Section 1 · Basic 初级基础

万用表达一览

- ☐ **It's one thing... and quite another** ……是两码事；……是一回事……是另外一回事（说明做一件事是合理的，做另外一件事却是很不合理的）
- ☐ **one memory stands out** 有一个记忆特别深刻
- ☐ **treat me like one of their own** 当成家人看待，不把我当外人

万用表达详解

1. **It's one thing... and quite another...**

   释 It's one matter doing this, but a very different matter doing that/often used like this: It is reasonable to do this...but very unreasonable to do that... ……是两码事；……是一回事……是另外一回事（说明做一件事是合理的，做另外一件事却是很不合理的）

   例 It's one thing visiting that country but quite another living there.

   去那个国家旅游是一回事，住在那儿又是另外一回事了。

2. **one memory stands out**

   释 one memory is quite vivid/unique 有一个记忆特别深刻

   例 One memory, in particular, stands out. That was the time we hiked up the mountain.

有一个记忆特别深刻，那是我们徒步上山的时候。

3. **treat me like one of their own**

释 treat me like a family member/like one of their compatriots/ countrymen 当成家人看待，不把我当外人

例 She treated him like one of her own.

她把他当成自己家人看待。

🗨 实用对话场景

John: So how was Paris?

Selina: Fascinating!

John: In what way?

Selina: The people for one thing. They come from all over and speak and behave in so many different ways.

John: What's so special about that? We learned about that in geography class.

Selina: *It's one thing* learning about foreign peoples and cultures from a book and *quite another* seeing them with your own eyes. It's much more complex.

John: I suppose you're right. So what was your most interesting memory of Paris?

Selina: That's hard. *One memory stands out* though. Spending a whole afternoon in the Spanish Quarter in Paris, eating delicious food and feeling so at home. The people there *treated me like one of their own*.

John: Well, you can't get that experience from reading books.

Selina: You got that right!

约翰：巴黎怎么样？

赛琳娜：迷人！

约翰：体现在哪些方面？

赛琳娜：首先体现在人上，他们来自五湖四海，言谈举止也各不相同。

约翰：那有什么特别？我们在地理课上都学过了。

赛琳娜：从书本上了解外国人文是一回事，亲眼看到又是另外一回事。后者复杂多了。

约翰：我想你说得没错。那么关于巴黎，你最有趣的记忆是什么？

赛琳娜：这很难回答，不过有一个记忆最深刻。那次我整个下午都待在巴黎的西语区，吃着好吃的东西，感觉就像在家一样。那里的人把我当作自己人一样看待。

约翰：嗯，我们无法从书本中得到那种体验。

赛琳娜：你说得对极了！

跨文化交际小常识

　　在美国，车辆和行人都是靠右侧通行，但在爱尔兰、苏格兰、英格兰、澳大利亚、新西兰、新加坡，以及日本等国都是靠左侧通行。当习惯右侧通行的人到规定左侧通行的国家时，走路和开车都可能发生危险，反之亦然。到了行驶习惯不同于自己国家的地方时，多年养成的走路和开车习惯会"背叛"你。习惯右侧走路的人，趋向于在右侧开车，当他们走到十字路口时，趋向于向左看，而实际上车辆是从另一边来的。在两种系统交接的地方，如英吉利海峡，经常发生交通事故，因为司机和行人常忘记通行差别。最好的解决方法是不开车，步行通过路口前，先向两个方向都看一看。

　　据英国路透社报道，伦敦电动出租车已经开始运行。这种电动出租车尽管外表还是之前的黑色，但现在已成为电动，而且配置天窗，提供手机充电和车内Wi-Fi功能。乘车价格与之前柴油出租车相同，这也意味着乘客可以在不增加费用的情况下实现环保出行。据报道，隶属于中国吉利（Geely）旗下的伦敦电动汽车公司（London Electric Vehicle Company）首席执行官克里斯古比（Chris Gubbey）表示：

"这仍是典型的伦敦黑色出租车，但这一切却又都焕然一新。作为一款新能源电动出租车，其采用了全新的纯铝车身结构，并搭载配有增程器的电动发动机，最为重要的是，它绿色环保。"虽然升级一套全新的电动车轮将会花费出租车司机大约5.5万英镑，但平均每周也将节省大约100磅的燃油费用。

读书笔记

Section 2 ◆ Intermediate 中级进阶

万用表达一览

- [ ] **From what I heard...** 我听说，据我所知……
- [ ] **Get this!** 想象一下！（如果可以的话）试着领会这个！（表示告诉某人某个惊喜、吃惊的消息）
- [ ] **We could go on and on.** 我们可以说个不停。
- [ ] **That's for sure!** 那是肯定的！

万用表达详解

1. **From what I heard...**

   释 based on what I've heard/According to what I have heard 我听说，据我所知

   例 From what I heard, he got everything he deserved.
   我听说他得到了应有的惩罚。

2. **Get this!**

   释 Imagine this; try to grasp this (if you can)/expressed when telling some one something that will surprise them. 想象一下！（如果可以的话）试着领会这个！（表示告诉某人某个惊喜、吃惊的消息）

   例 Get this! Scientists have just discovered a new way to make glass.
   你想象一下！科学家已经发现了一种制造玻璃的新方法。

3. **We could go on and on.**

   释 We could continue to talk about it. 我们可以说个不停。

   例 We could go on and on about how awful things are, but what good would it (that) do?

我们可以滔滔不绝地说事情有多么糟糕，但那有什么用呢?

4. That's for sure!

释 That's certain! 那是肯定的!

例 A: We're doing better than before.

我们做得比以前好。

B: That's for sure!

那是肯定的!

实用对话场景

John: We were discussing body language in school today.

Selina: Body language? You mean gestures and stuff like that?

John: Exactly. Our teacher was telling us that there are 700,000 forms of body language in the world. We talked about curious gestures I had never heard of before.

Selina: Such as?

John: Well, for example people in some parts of Greece, Bulgaria and Turkey nod their heads to indicate "no".

Selina: That's strange. **From what I heard**, tapping your nose in England means "confidential", but it means "Watch out!" in Italy .

John: And then there are cultures in Philippines, North America and South America that point with their lips, like we point with our fingers.

Selina: That is weird. But **get this!** The curled index finger into the thumb sign or "OK" sign means fine to you and me, right? But it's "worthless" in France, and it's considered an insult in Greece, Brazil, Italy, Turkey, and Russia. Oh, yeah. I almost forgot! That "thumb up" sign, meaning "Great!", is an insult in most African countries.

John: Wow! ***We could go on and on.*** There's just so much to learn about body language, and so much to think about.

Selina: ***That's for sure!***

约翰：今天我们在学校讨论肢体语言。

赛琳娜：肢体语言？你指的是手势之类的东西？

约翰：正是。我们老师告诉我们，世界上有 700000 种肢体语言。我们讨论了一些我以前从未听过的奇怪的手势。

赛琳娜：比如说呢？

约翰：比如说在希腊、保加利亚和土耳其的一些地方，人们点头表示"不"。

赛琳娜：这真奇怪。我听说，在英国，轻拍鼻子表示"保密"，但在意大利，则表示"小心！"。

约翰：还有，在菲律宾、北美和南美有一些文化群体，用嘴唇指方向，就和我们用手指指方向一样。

赛琳娜：真怪，不过想想这个！把大拇指和食指卷曲成"O"形状或"OK"手势，对于你我来说意思是"好的"，对吧？但在法国它的意思是"没价值"，在希腊、巴西、意大利、土耳其和俄罗斯被当作一种侮辱。啊，我差点忘记了，竖起拇指的手势，意思是"好"，而在大部分非洲国家，被当作一种侮辱。

约翰：哇！我们可以举出无数的例子，肢体语言就是有很多东西可以学习和思考啊。

赛琳娜：那当然！

跨文化交际小常识

虽然汽车给人类提供了更舒适和便捷的出行方式，加速了经济的发展，但同时也带来了一些负面效应。交通事故就是其中最严重、危害最大的负面效应之一。世界各国都对交通事故的预防及对策倾注了大量的人力、物力和财力。近年来，西方许多国家的交通事故发生率已趋于平稳，但在我国却一直处于上升趋势，每年的交通事故死亡人数也居于世界首位。事实上，中国有句古话"无规矩不成方圆"（Nothing can be accomplished without norms or standards.），但在交通规矩方面，依然有不少人侥幸地认为规矩是人定的，甚至还有人以不守规矩为荣。

读书笔记

Section 3 Advanced 高级飞跃

万用表达一览

☐ **to indicate** 表示，指示

☐ **Believe it or not** 无论你相信与否（事实是……）

☐ **use/follow conventional** 使用传统的，按照常规的

☐ **make up for it in other ways/make up for it some other way** 用其他方式弥补

☐ **subtle** 微妙的，含蓄的

☐ **may not even be obvious to** 甚至可能不明显，甚至很难被领会

万用表达详解

1. **to indicate**

   释 to signal 表示，指示

   例 She waved her hand to indicate that she wanted to see me.
   她冲我挥挥手，表示她想见我。

2. **Believe it or not**

   释 Whether you believe it or not, it's the truth/it's a fact... 无论你相信与否（事实是……）

   例 Believe it or not, I've never heard of that rule.
   不管你相不相信，我从来没有听说过那项规定。

3. **use/follow conventional**

   释 do what most people do 使用传统的，按照常规的

   例 She used conventional gestures to communicate with me.
   她用约定俗成的手势与我交流。

4. **make up for it in other ways/make up for it some other way**

   释 do something else to compensate for 用其他方式弥补

例 He's not very sociable, but I think he means well. He makes up for it in other ways.

他不善交际，但我认为他的用意是好的。他用其他的方式在弥补。

5. **subtle**

释 not direct/not obvious　微妙的，含蓄的

例 He made a subtle move backwards, indicating that he wasn't in agreement.

他向后稍微退了一步，表示他不同意此事。

6. **may not even be obvious to**

释 may not be clearly visible/noticeable　甚至可能不明显，甚至很难被领会

例 Adults lose their sense of hearing over time. It may not even be obvious to them.

随着时间的推移，大人们会渐渐失去听觉，但他们甚至没觉察到。

实用对话场景

John: There's universal body language we all understand.

Selina: Right. Most people nod **to indicate** "yes", shake their heads from side to side to indicate "no". But **believe it or not**, not everyone in the world **uses** these **conventional gestures**. In Bulgaria people move their heads up and down to indicate "no" and from left to right to indicate "yes". Strange, isn't it?

John: I've seen Indians wobble their heads when they're talking. It can sometimes get very confusing.

Selina: Korean women don't usually shake hands with men. Middle Eastern men stand very close to each other. The French, Russians and Arabs kiss each other on the cheeks.

John: Yes. And in Central and South American countries, people are quite physical, when they meet each other... the Chinese not so much.

Selina: But people that don't wear their hearts on their sleeves, so to speak, **make up for it in other ways**. They enjoy eating and celebrating together quite often.

John: Our body language can be quite **subtle** too. It **may not even be obvious to** the person we're talking to.

约翰：有一些我们都知道的通用肢体语言。

赛琳娜：没错，大多数人用点头表示"是"，左右摇头表示"不"。但信不信由你，世界上并不是所有人都使用这些常规的肢体语言的。在保加利亚，人们用上下点头表示"不"，用左右摇头表示"是"。很奇怪吧？

约翰：我看到印度人说话时总是摇头，有时候会让人感到很困惑。

赛琳娜：韩国女人通常不跟男人握手，中东的男人相互间站得很近，法国、俄罗斯和阿拉伯人见面时互相亲吻脸颊。

约翰：是的，在中南美洲国家，人们彼此见面时有相当多的肢体动作，而中国人则较少用肢体语言。

赛琳娜：但可以说，那些不轻易表露自己的人，就会用其他的方式来表达，比如他们喜欢经常一起吃饭、庆祝。

约翰：我们的肢体语言也是相当微妙的，有时连谈话中的另一方也很难领会到。

跨文化交际小常识

　　自驾游这个词汇最早出现在20世纪的美国，被视为一种充满个性的旅游方式。如今，它已成为欧美发达国家最重要的旅游方式之一。每年的12月底到1月中旬，是美国人最重要的外出旅游度假时间。全美汽车协会估计至少有5000万美国人选择自驾游，占总人口的六分之一，更占到出游人数的一半以上，美国也因此被称为"车轮上旅行的国家"。

Section 1 Basic 初级基础

📱 万用表达一览

☐ **don't pay much attention to** 不会非常关注 / 关心 / 留意 / 在意
☐ **read up on** 仔细研究，熟读
☐ **No wonder/It's no wonder...** 怪不得
☐ **I was just beginning to think** 我原先还以为
☐ **feel like a guinea pig/a canary in a coal mine** 感觉像一只小白鼠

📱 万用表达详解

1. **don't pay much attention to**

   释 I don't care about/listen to... 我不会非常关注 / 关心 / 留意 /
   在意

   例 I don't pay much attention to that gossip mongering any
   more. It's so uncouth.

   我不会再关心那些八卦了，那很俗。

2. **read up on**

   释 read about a subject matter to become more familiar with
   it 仔细研究，熟读

   例 I enjoy reading up on the latest science articles in *Astronomy
   Today*.

   我喜欢仔细研读《当代天文学》里面的最新科普文章。

3. **No wonder/It's no wonder...**

   释 It's no surprise then that 怪不得

例 You've spent the last of your savings. No wonder you're broke.

你已经用完你最后的积蓄了。怪不得你破产了。

4. **I was just beginning to think...**

释 I was just starting to think/I was beginning to wonder 我原先
还以为

例 Good thing your idea was correct. I was just beginning to
think you were mad.

你的想法是正确的，真好。我原先还以为你疯了呢。

5. **feel like a guinea pig/a canary in a coal mine**

释 feel like a person on which something is being tested for the
first time 感觉像一只小白鼠

例 I felt like a guinea pig, when my biology teacher asked me to
stand in front of the class to show my teeth.

当生物老师让我站在教室前露出牙齿的时候，我感觉自己就像
一只小白鼠。

实用对话场景

Bob: I've never seen so many cameras and monitors in a department
store before.

Tina: You're very observant. Most people ***don't pay much attention
to*** them.

Bob: I was ***reading up on*** some of the high-tech equipment that
stores have these days.

Tina: Ah! ***No wonder! I was just beginning to think*** you had been
watching too many spy movies.

Bob: So here's what's interesting. Many leading department stores
do research on their customers, so they observe customers
while they're shopping.

Tina: Observe? I'm starting to ***feel like a guinea pig*** in a research lab.

Bob: Don't worry. It's harmless. They simply watch customers as they shop, to find out what customers like and don't like, what they notice and don't notice.

Tina: That's easy. Just put everything I need in the same area and I'm happy. Don't put shoes on the first floor and pants on the third floor. Oh yeah, and hire plenty of cashiers, so we don't have to line up behind just one on each floor.

Bob: Well, someone's listening, I'm sure.

鲍勃：我以前从没见过一家商店安装这么多摄像头和监视器。

蒂娜：你很善于观察啊，很多人都没有留意到那些呢。

鲍勃：我好好研究过现在商店里的一些高科技设备。

蒂娜：难怪。我还以为你看了太多侦探电影呢。

鲍勃：有趣的是，很多大型的百货公司都会调查他们的顾客，所以他们会在顾客购物时观察他们。

蒂娜：观察？我开始觉得自己是实验室里的小白鼠了。

鲍勃：别担心，那并没有恶意。他们观察顾客购物只是为了知道顾客喜欢和不喜欢什么，注意和不注意什么而已。

蒂娜：很简单嘛。把我需要的东西都放在同一区域，我就开心了。不要把鞋子放在一楼，裤子放在三楼。哦对，还要多请一些收银员，那我们就不用在每个楼层的一个收银台前排一条长长的队了。

鲍勃：嗯，我敢肯定有人在听着呢。

跨文化交际小常识

在美国，驾照不仅是开车的资格证明文件，更是一种被广泛使用的身份证件。出门在外，买车、租车、买保险、住旅馆、开支票、签信用卡等，几乎都能用到它。相对来说，在美国申请驾照是一件很容易的事情。与中国一样，在美国考驾照也是由笔试和路考两部分组成的，至于考试内容和难度则是由各个州的相关部门自己把握。关于笔试，主要考查交通规则。考生可以到附近的机动车辆管理局（DMV，Department of Motor Vehicles）索取一本该州汽车驾驶规则。当交通规则准备好之后，就可以申请笔试了。笔试合格后，考生即可领到一张限期一年的学习驾驶执照（Instruction Permit）。一年期限内，一般有三次路考（road test）机会。有了学习驾驶执照，就可以找已有驾照的家人或朋友学习，或者花钱去驾校学习。路考时，必须要有持有驾照的家人或朋友陪同。

读书笔记

Section 2 · Intermediate 中级进阶

万用表达一览

- [ ] **I've always wondered why...** 我一直在想，为什么……
- [ ] **imagine** 想象
- [ ] **Granted!** 同意!
- [ ] **What does that have to do with...?** 那跟这有什么关系?
- [ ] **Now you have it!** 现在你懂了!

万用表达详解

1. **I've always wondered why...**

   释 I have always been curious/interested to know why... 我一直在想，为什么……

   例 I've always wondered why it's taken so long for humans to evolve.

   我一直在想，为什么人类用了那么长时间来进化。

2. **imagine**

   释 ① picture/visualize 想象; ② suppose/assume 想（猜测）

   例 Wow! Imagine spending the rest of your life there.

   哇! 设想一下，在那儿度过余生。

3. **Granted!**

   释 Agreed! 同意!

   例 Granted! I was a little preoccupied. I should have been more considerate.

   同意! 我有点太专注于其他的事了，应该要考虑周到一些的。

4. **What does that have to do with...?**

   释 What is the connection between this and that? 那跟这有什么

关系？

例 What does that have to do with anything? We're talking about something completely different. You're confusing the issues.

那跟这一切有什么关系？我们说的完全是两码事，你弄混了。

5. **Now you have it!**

释 Now you've got it!/Now you understand!/Now you see! 现在你懂了！

例 A: Wow. I just solved the equation.

哇，我刚刚解出了那道方程式。

B: Now you have it!

现在你懂了！

实用对话场景

Bob: ***I've always wondered*** why there are so many security cameras in department stores these days.

Tina: Well, I ***imagine*** it's because some people try to steal things.

Bob: OK. ***Granted***! That's one reason. But then there's another reason.

Tina: What's that?

Bob: So they can observe customer behavior.

Tina: Customer behavior? What does that ***have to do with*** shopping?

Bob: No. You misunderstand me. I'm not talking about good or bad behavior. I'm talking about what customers do, when they're deciding whether to buy or not to buy an item.

Tina: I see. So you're saying department stores may be studying a customer's posture, facial expressions, even the way he or she touches or handles an item.

Bob: ***Now you have it***!

鲍勃：我常常想，为什么现在商场里有那么多监控摄像头。

蒂娜：嗯，我想那是因为有些人企图偷东西。

鲍勃：好吧。同意！那是一个原因，但还有另外的原因。

蒂娜：是什么？

鲍勃：就是，他们能观察顾客的行为。

蒂娜：顾客的行为？那跟购物有什么关系？

鲍勃：不，你误解我的意思了。我不是在说好或不好的行为，我说的是顾客在决定要不要买一件商品的时候会做些什么。

蒂娜：我懂了。所以你是说商店可能会研究顾客的姿势、面部表情，甚至是他们摸或者拿商品的方式。

鲍勃：现在你弄明白了！

跨文化交际小常识

在伦敦街头，出租汽车随处可见。你只需在用车时轻声叫一声，就会有出租车应声而至。伦敦的出租汽车是清一色的老式"奥斯汀"牌汽车，看上去又高大又笨重，这使它们在川流不息的车流中极易辨认。这种黑色的出租汽车乘坐起来非常舒适。它们身高1.7米，比普通小汽车高出一截。车内，司机与乘客是隔开的，司机旁边的位置不设座位，而是用来存放乘客的小件物品。汽车后排可坐四个人，身前还设有折叠椅，打开之后还可坐两人。这样，亲朋好友五六人外出，只需叫一辆出租车就足够了。需要注意的是，既然这种出租车可以随叫随停，那就意味着它们的收费也不菲。一般情况下，英国的这种"黑色老爷出租车"，其收费是预约标准的1.5倍。

Section 3 Advanced 高级飞跃

万用表达一览

☐ **We tend to...** 我们倾向于……

☐ **such a "hot" topic among** 在……之间……是非常热门的话题

☐ **The short answer is...** 简单地说就是

☐ **answers to age-old questions** 回答古老（由来已久）的问题

☐ **The issue here is...** 这里的问题是，问题在于……

☐ **read subtle body language** 看懂微妙的肢体语言

☐ **buy into** 相信

☐ **avoid misunderstandings** 避免误解

☐ **I can't vouch for all of it.** 我不能保证全部（内容）的真实性／正确性。

☐ **make for** ……有助于，走向

☐ **engage people in face-to-face conversations** 进行面对面交流

☐ **greatly expand** 大幅增加，极大地扩大

万用表达详解

1. **We tend to...**

   释 We are inclined to... 我们倾向于……

   例 We tend to increasingly ignore bad behavior.

   我们有越来越忽视不良行为的倾向。

2. **such a "hot" topic among**

   释 such a controversial topic among 在……之间……是非常热门的话题

   例 The economy is a "hot" topic among people of all ages these days.

   现在，无论是在什么年龄段，经济都是一个热门话题。

3. **The short answer is...**

   释 a brief answer/put simply 简单地说就是

例 A: How can I improve my English fluency more rapidly?

我怎样才能更快地提高自己的英语口语流利度？

B: The short answer is practice.

简单地说就是练习。

4. **answers to age-old questions**

释 answer questions that have been asked for ages/a long time

回答古老（由来已久）的问题

例 Scientists have been delving into some age-old questions and have come up with some surprising answers.

科学家们深入研究由来已久的问题，并给出了一些惊人的答案。

5. **The issue here is...**

释 the matter at hand is 这里的问题是，问题在于

例 The issue here is whether or not there's a market for this product.

这里的问题在于这种产品是否有市场。

6. **read subtle body language**

释 read body language that is not very noticeable 看懂微妙的肢体语言

例 It takes years to become a master at reading subtle body language.

想成为解读微妙肢体语言的大师，要花几年的时间。

7. **buy into**

释 accept/believe 相信

例 I could tell he wasn't buying into the plan. He had serious doubts about it.

我能看出他不相信这个计划，他对此很怀疑。

8. **avoid misunderstandings**

释 try not to cause misunderstandings 避免误解

例 We should try to make an effort to get to know each other better. That will help us all avoid misunderstandings in our day-to-day dealings with each other.

我们应该努力去更好地了解对方，这可以帮助我们在日常工作中避免误解。

9. **I can't vouch for all of it.**

释 I can't guarantee the authenticity/correctness of all of it. 我不能保证全部（内容）的真实性/正确性。

例 A: What's your take on this new book, claiming we're all in for some nasty global weather?

你对这本新书有什么看法？书上说我们会遇到一些恶劣的全球性气候。

B: I can't vouch for all of it.

我不能保证全部内容的真实性。

10. **make for**

释 promote/have the effect of... ……有助于，走向

例 The invention of gunpowder by the Chinese is a decisive moment in world history and makes for interesting reading as well.

中国人发明的火药在世界历史上具有里程碑意义，也给阅读提供了有趣的素材。

11. **engage people in face-to-face conversations**

释 have face-to-face conversations with people 进行面对面交流

例 Following a huge spike in online chatting, psychologists are advising people to engage in more face-to-face conversations.

随着网上聊天的飞速发展，心理学家建议人们多进行面对面的交流。

12. **greatly expand**

释 greatly increase 大幅增加，极大地扩大

例 The Internet has greatly expanded our knowledge but has also undermined our sense of certainty.

网络极大地拓展了我们的知识，但也加深了我们的不确定感。

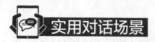 **实用对话场景**

Bob: We are all communicators. Wouldn't you agree?

Tina: Yes. But we communicate in different ways. **We tend to** use more body language than verbal language to express ourselves.

Bob: So that's why body language is **such a "hot" topic among** scientists, consumer research groups, and people working in sales and marketing. But tell me, why do you think it's so important?

Tina: **The short answer is** revenue. With more and more money devoted to consumer research, scientists can help find **answers to the age-old questions:** Why do we buy? Why don't we buy? Companies and department stores then use that research to induce customers to spend more. But **the issue here is** not just about buying a commodity. It's also about communication.

Bob: I see. So, if I know and understand all the signals a person makes, then I can understand the unspoken communication and respond in the right way.

Tina: Yes. Most of us can't **read subtle body language** very well. This subtle body language will tell us whether a person will buy or not, **buy into** or not buy into what you're selling or proposing.

Bob: It can also tell us if someone is being truthful or lying to us.

Tina: Right. I for one, would encourage people to learn as much as they can about body language around the world. This can help them **avoid** or even eliminate **misunderstandings** that arise in day-to-day dealings with people.

Bob: There's a lot of popular literature about body language and interpretations of body language out there.

Tina: I know. **I can't vouch for all of it**, but some of it can **make for** interesting readings. The best way to really understand body language is to **engage people in face-to-face conversations** as much as possible. Traveling will also **_greatly expand_** your knowledge on the subject.

Bob: I think that's really useful advice.

鲍勃：我们都是交流者，难道你不同意吗？

蒂娜：同意，但我们用不同的方式沟通。相比有声语言，我们更倾向于用肢体语言来表达自己。

鲍勃：这就是肢体语言在科学家、消费者调查团体及销售和市场营销人员当中如此热门的原因。但告诉我，为什么你觉得它们很重要呢？

蒂娜：简单地说就是收入。随着越来越多的钱投入市场调查当中，科学家们可以找到这些由来已久的问题的答案：我们为什么买？我们为什么不买？然后，各类公司和百货商店都在利用这类市场调查来诱导顾客多购物。但这里要讨论的不只是购买某个商品的事情，还涉及交流的问题。

鲍勃：我明白了，所以如果我能掌握并理解一个人所发出的信号，那么我就能听懂这些无声的信息，并正确地做出回应了。

蒂娜：是的，我们大多数人都不是很懂微妙的身体语言。这种微妙的身体语言会告诉我们一个人是否愿意购买、是否相信你向他们推销或建议购买的东西。

鲍勃：这也可以告诉我们一个人是在说真话还是在说谎。

蒂娜：对，我个人会鼓励人们尽可能多地学习世界各地的肢体语言，这有助于让人们避免甚至消除在日常交流中产生误解。

鲍勃：市面上有很多关于肢体语言及其诠释的通俗文学。

蒂娜：我知道。虽然我不能保证它们全部都真实，但其中有不少是有趣的读物。真正地理解肢体语言的最好的方法是尽量多地进行面对面的交流，旅游也能够大幅增长你这方面的知识。

鲍勃：我觉得这建议很管用。

跨文化交际小常识

从每24小时运送的乘客数量、所覆盖的面积、线路数、车站数量以及站与站之间距离等方面来衡量，世界地铁第一的位置当属伦敦地铁（London Underground）。它是欧洲最大、也是最古老的地铁网络，从1863年开始运营，全长253英里(约合407公里)，每年运送乘客近10亿人次。巴黎地铁（Paris Metro）也是世界最好的地铁之一，和它的高效相比，乘客们更为津津乐道的是每个站点独特的艺术设计。纽约地铁（New York City Subway，简称NYCS）的好评度有所下降是因为它是世界上票价最贵的地铁之一，也是最不安全和最不卫生的地铁。近年来亚洲地铁在世界的排名有所上升，包括有282个站点的东京地铁（Tokyo Metro）和堪称世界上最拥挤的地铁之一的首尔地铁（Seoul Subway）。

读书笔记

Unit 3

Food & Drink
食品和饮料

万用表达一览

☐ **pay more attention** 更关注
☐ **more talk** 越来越多的讨论
☐ **resistant to** 对……有抵抗力的；耐……的
☐ **Scary stuff!** 真吓人！

万用表达详解

1. **pay more attention**

   释 look closely at 更关注

   例 We should pay more attention to our weight.

   我们应该更关注自己的体重。

2. **more talk**

   释 more discussion 越来越多的讨论

   例 There's more talk these days of encouraging native culture and festivals.

   现在有越来越多倡导传统文化和节日的言论。

3. **resistant to**

   释 unresponsive to 对……有抵抗力的；耐……的

   例 Scientists have found that eating meat has made us more resistant to antibiotics.

   科学家们已经发现，吃肉类食品使我们对抗生素具有更强的耐药性。

4. **Scary stuff!**

释 Frightening matter! 真吓人！

例 A: I watched a program on TV about history's most violent and destructive volcanoes, such as Krakatoa Island and Mt. (Mount) Tambora in Indonesia. Their eruptions had an enormous impact on the earth's climate.

我看了一档电视节目，介绍了历史上最有威力、破坏性最强的火山，比如喀拉喀托岛和印尼的坦博拉火山。它们的爆发对地球气候有巨大的影响。

B: Wow! Scary stuff!

哇，真吓人！

实用对话场景

Kate: We were discussing the food pyramid in class today.

Jack: You mean all the food groups?

Kate: Yeah, but in the shape of a pyramid.

Jack: I see. So, what should we be eating?

Kate: Lots of vege and fruit, for one thing. Fish, of course.

Jack: What about meat? Is it still OK to eat pork, beef, lamb, chicken and so on?

Kate: Yes, but not too much of it. People these days should **pay more attention** to their hearts and cholesterol levels. There's also **more talk** these days of antibiotic resistance to infections because of the meat we consume.

Jack: Yeah. I've heard about that... Bacteria, called "superbugs" that are **resistant to** all known antibiotics.

Kate: Yeah. **Scary stuff!**

凯特：今天在课堂上我们讨论了食物金字塔。

杰克：你指的是全部的食物组？

凯特：是啊，不过是以金字塔的形式（呈现）的。

杰克：我懂了。那我们应该吃什么？

凯特：首先，要吃很多蔬菜和水果，当然还有鱼。

杰克：肉呢？还可以吃猪肉、牛肉、羊肉、鸡肉等吗？

凯特：可以，但不能吃太多。今天人们应该更关注他们的心脏和胆固醇水平。也有更多人说人体产生抗生素耐药性，是因为我们食用的肉类食品。

杰克：嗯，我听说过那种叫"超级细菌"的细菌，对所有已知的抗生素都有耐药性。

凯特：是啊，真吓人！

🎒 跨文化交际小常识

　　公交车是纽约市民和学生最常用的代步工具。纽约市五个区，共有3700辆公交车，行驶在200条线路上，每一区的公交车分别用该区英文名的第一个字母进行标注，如：曼哈顿Manhattan——M；皇后区Queens——Q；布鲁克林 Brooklyn——B；布朗士Bronx——BX；史坦顿岛Staten Island——S。字母后面的数字即该区某一线路的公交车。大多数巴士不跨区行驶，少数例外，但各区均有快车通往曼哈顿。在公交上，乘客可以通过两种方式示意司机停车：点击两个车窗之间的一个胶带似的黄色长条形橡皮开关（Tape Strip），或者点击扶手栏上的停车按钮（Stop）。在一些公交车门上，也会有一个黄色长条形橡皮开关。如果点按该开关，门会自动打开。

Section 2 — Intermediate 中级进阶

📲 万用表达一览

- ☐ **pick up** 买东西
- ☐ **have a good diet** 有良好的饮食
- ☐ **get all … I need** 获得我需要的一切……
- ☐ **hard to tell** 很难说，很难分辨，很难知道
- ☐ **take … for granted** 当作理所当然
- ☐ **build up** 增加
- ☐ **not to mention** 更不用说，而且
- ☐ **just to be sure** 确定 / 确认一下
- ☐ **in that case** 假如那样的话，既然是那样

📲 万用表达详解

1. **pick up**

   释 buy something 买东西

   例 I'm picking up some things from the shop. Do you want to come?
   我要去店里买些东西，你要一起去吗？

2. **have a good diet**

   释 eat healthily/eat all the right foods/consume all the proper foods and nutrients/"eat right"/"eat healthy" 有良好的饮食

   例 A: We do our best to maintain a good diet. Is it perfect?
   我们尽量坚持良好的饮食，这样够了吧？

   B: Not by a long shot!
   还远着呢！

3. **get all… I need**

   释 receive all the assistance I need 获得我需要的一切……

   例 I get all the help I need from my family.

我从家人那儿得到了所需的帮助。

4. **hard to tell**

   释 difficult to know... 很难说，很难分辨，很难知道

   例 It's hard to tell if he's being honest or not.

   很难分辨他老不老实。

5. **take... for granted**

   释 think that things/people we enjoy (like/love) will always be that way/be around 当作理所当然

   例 We take our families for granted for far too long. We need to stand on our own two feet sooner or later.

   一直以来我们都把家人（的帮助）当成理所当然的事情，（其实）我们迟早要靠自己。

6. **build up**

   释 to increase in amount of quantity 增加

   例 Wax had built up in his ears over a long period.

   他耳朵里的耳垢越来越多。

7. **not to mention**

   释 too obvious to mention 更不用说，而且

   例 Many so-called historical feature films today are factually incorrect, not to mention moronic.

   现在很多所谓的历史片都是错误百出的，而且很蠢。

8. **just to be sure**

   释 just to be on the safe side 确定 / 确认一下

   例 Just to be sure, you don't take sugar in your tea, right?

   确认一下，你的茶里不加糖，对吧?

9. **in that case**

   释 well, then 假如那样的话，既然是那样

   例 A: I don't want to discuss it any more.

我不想再讨论了。

B: Well, in that case, the matter is closed.

这样的话，就到此为止了。

实用对话场景

Kate: I'm going to **pick up** some vitamins from the store.

Jack: Do you take vitamins?

Kate: Sure. Don't you?

Jack: Not really. I **have a good diet** and **get all** the vitamins **I need**. Unless my doctor prescribes them, I don't take them.

Kate: Yeah. Well, the thing is, it's **hard to tell** if we're getting the proper amounts of all the vitamins we need. I just take one multi-vitamin tablet a day. I don't abuse them. That's dangerous.

Jack: Glad to hear it. I agree, though, that we sometimes **take our health and diet for granted.**

Kate: Someone I know broke his arm recently, and the doctor told him he was calcium deficient. He couldn't believe it. He drank milk, ate cheese and thought he had a calcium-rich diet. But he was wrong.

Jack: Yeah. These days, eating all the right food may not even be enough for your body. Vegetables and fruits, for example, grow so quickly that plants can't **build up** enough vitamins by the time they're harvested.

Kate: So that explains all these interest in juicers and eating more fruits and vege in concentrated form, **not to mention** popping lots of vitamin tablets **just to be sure**.

Jack: I see your point. Well **in that case**, pick up some multi-vitamin tablets for me too, if you don't mind.

Kate: Not at all. Glad to.

凯特：我打算去店里买点维生素。

杰克：你吃维生素吗？

凯特：当然。你不吃吗？

杰克：不怎么吃。我有良好的饮食习惯，摄取了所需的各种维生素。除非医生给我开维生素，不然我不会吃。

凯特：嗯。问题是，我们很难判定自己是否补够了人体所需的各种维生素。我每天只服用一片多元维生素，我不滥服，那很危险。

杰克：很高兴听到你这样说。不过，我也同意，有时我们把自己的健康和饮食当成理所当然的事。

凯特：我认识一个人，他最近手臂骨折了。医生告诉他，他缺钙，他都不敢相信，他觉得自己喝牛奶，吃奶酪，有富含钙质的饮食，但他错了。

杰克：是啊，现在即使吃了所有合适的食物，对你的身体来说也许还是不够的，因为蔬菜和水果长得太快，即便到收割的时候，也还没储存足够的维生素。

凯特：这就解释了人们为什么热衷于用榨汁机、吃更多浓缩的蔬果。更不用说，经常服用大量的维生素片了，仅仅是为了有个保障。

杰克：我明白你的意思了。既然这样，如果你不介意的话，也帮我买一些多元维生素片吧。

凯特：一点都不介意，很乐意呢。

跨文化交际小常识

①在乘飞机的前一天，应该保证充足的睡眠。②在起飞前半小时口服晕机药，可以在5~6小时内不呕吐。③登机前既不可空腹，也不可饱食。④尽量选择距离发动机较远且靠近窗户的座位。⑤视线尽量放远，看远处的云和山脉等，不要看近处的云。⑥在飞机起飞、转弯、下降以及遇到较大幅度的颠簸时，尽量减少活动，尤其要固定头部，不能转动。⑦晕机比较严重引起机体失水时，要及时补充生理盐水。

Section 3　Advanced 高级飞跃

万用表达一览

- [ ] **firm believer in** 对……的深信者，坚信……的人
- [ ] **a first step to** 第一步，首先要做的事情
- [ ] **in this day and age** 如今，这个时代
- [ ] **shouldn't be surprised** 不应感到奇怪，这并不奇怪
- [ ] **thanks to** 由于，多亏
- [ ] **hotly debated** 激烈地争论
- [ ] **If you ask me** 如果你想知道我的观点，如果你想听我的观点
- [ ] **factors have contributed** 这些因素导致（促成）了
- [ ] **That's all I'm saying** 这就是我想说的，仅此而已
- [ ] **in a nutshell** 简言之，总而言之
- [ ] **Not quite.** 不全是。/ 未必见得。
- [ ] **better off in terms of** 在……方面富裕多了（日子好起来了）
- [ ] **As for... nothing beats** 至于……没有什么更胜于
- [ ] **Come to think of it** 经你这么一提醒，我想起来了
- [ ] **I can tell you first-hand** 我可以直接告诉你，我可以凭我自己的经验告诉你
- [ ] **You can rest assured...** 你可以放心

万用表达详解

1. **firm believer in**

   释 I believe strongly that... 对……的深信者，坚信……的人

   例 I'm a firm believer in people standing on their own two feet.
   我坚信自食其力的人。

2. **a first step to**

   释 a first move 第一步，首先要做的事情

例 As a first step, we should always wash our hands thoroughly before sitting down to eat.

首先，在坐下吃饭前，我们要彻底把手洗干净。

3. **in this day and age**

释 in today's world 如今，这个时代

例 In this day and age, we have to learn to be more tolerant of each other.

在如今这个时代，我们必须学会更加宽以待人。

4. **shouldn't be surprised**

释 should not think of it as unusual/should not come as a surprise 不应感到奇怪，这并不奇怪

例 We shouldn't be surprised if he ups and leaves some day/one day.

如果有一天，他一去不复返了，我们也不奇怪。

5. **thanks to**

释 because of 由于，多亏

例 Thanks to my upbringing and education, I have no problems getting ahead in life.

由于我受到的教养和教育，在生活中取得成功是不成问题的。

6. **hotly debated**

释 controversial 激烈地争论

例 Their motives for going to war have been hotly debated for years.

多年来他们发动战争的动机一直备受争议。

7. **If you ask me**

释 If you want my opinion on the matter 如果你想知道我的观点，如果你想听我的观点

例 If you ask me, you were very lucky. You were in the right place at the right time.

依我看，你运气很好，一切都像刻意安排的一样那么巧。

8. factors have contributed

释 the elements that helped (cause sth.) 这些因素导致（促成）了

例 We know all the factors that contributed to the financial crisis.
我们知道引发金融危机的各种因素。

9. That's all I'm saying.

释 I'm just saying this. That's all. 这就是我想说的，仅此而已

例 His comment was uncalled for. That's all I'm saying.
他的评论是不公正的，这就是我想说的。

10. in a nutshell

释 briefly speaking 简言之，总而言之

例 In a nutshell, we don't have the resources to continue the project.
总而言之，我们没有资源来继续这项工程。

11. Not quite.

释 Not exactly. 不全是。/ 未必见得。

例 A: Have you finished running errands yet?
你给别人跑完腿了吗？

B: Not quite. I still have a few more to do.
还没有，我还有一些事情要做。

12. better off in terms of

释 doing better in relation to... 在……方面富裕多了（日子好起来了）

例 A: You can't deny that we're better off in almost every way, compared to our ancestors.
你不能否认，同我们的祖先相比，我们在各方面都好多了。

B: In what way?
哪方面啊？

A: In terms of health, leisure time and the freedom to be what we want to be.

健康、休闲和自由选择自己想做的事情方面。

B: You have a point there.

你说得有道理。

13. As for... nothing beats

释 When it comes to... nothing is better than/In relation to... nothing is better than... 至于……没有什么更胜于

例 As for tennis tournaments, nothing beats Wimbledon.

至于网球大满贯比赛，没有什么比得上温布尔登国际网球锦标赛了。

14. Come to think of it

释 Now that you remind me/Now that I think about it/Now that I'm reminded/Now that you remind me, 经你这么一提醒，我想起来了

例 Come to think of it, that's not the first time I've heard that story.

我想起来了，这不是我第一次听到那个故事。

15. I can tell you first-hand

释 I can tell you from my own experience 我可以直接告诉你，我可以凭我自己的经验告诉你

例 I can tell you first-hand that the good old days weren't necessarily that great. Mind you, we did have more adventure growing up than kids do nowadays.

我可以凭经验告诉你，以前的日子并不一定就是那么好的。听着，和现在的孩子比起来，我们那会儿所经历的冒险的确要多得多。

16. You can rest assured...

释 You can be certain that... 你可以放心

例 You can rest assured that the neighborhood is very safe at night.

你可以放心，这附近晚上非常安全。

 **实用对话场景**

Kate: I'm a ***firm believer in*** choosing the right food, as ***a first step to*** a healthy diet.

Jack: I agree. I think ***in this day and age***, with so much processed food replacing traditional fresh produce, we ***shouldn't be surprised*** that so many young people are developing diseases we used to associate with the elderly.

Kate: Yes. Diabetes, for example, is now more common in teenagers than ever before, ***thanks to*** the over-consumption of fast food.

Jack: It's funny, isn't it? On the one hand, we're inundated with competing diet infomercials and the latest exercise machines, but at the same time we are encouraged to take life easy and live life to the full.

Kate: Good point. You know, food and how we grow it, process it and eat it, have been ***hotly debated for years.***

Jack: ***If you ask me***, I think the more rapid urbanization of the world and the higher costs of fresh farm produce, not to mention, smaller household budgets and changing lifestyles, have led to more competition, to feed larger and larger populations with cheaper and more easily prepared foods.

Kate: So you're blaming greater urbanization, higher food costs, smaller household budgets and changing lifestyles for our decline in health?

Jack: That's too simplistic. All these ***factors have contributed*** to our changing diets. ***That's all I'm saying.***

Kate: OK. So, ***in a nutshell***, we've left our traditional diets behind, and have completely embraced micro-wave ready meals.

Jack: ***Not quite***. But in some respects, we were ***better off in terms of*** our diets twenty or thirty years ago.

Kate: What about drinking? What should we be drinking?

Jack: **As for** drinking, **nothing beats** drinking lots of water. It refreshes, cools, cleans and nourishes our bodies.

Kate: Some say water is the ultimate cure-all.

Jack: I wouldn't go that far, but there is no doubt that we can't do without it.

Kate: **Come to think of it,** other drinks that are good for you include tea, especially green tea, flower tea and pu'er tea.

Jack: Absolutely correct. Maybe you think it's old-fashioned to drink tea, but I'm a firm believer in the curative and medicinal properties of tea. **I can tell you first-hand**, how drinking tea every day helped me. Even if you think it doesn't do anything for you, **you can rest assured** it's certainly not bad for you.

Kate: Wow, this conversation has certainly been very lively and very enlightening.

凯特：我深信选择正确的食物是健康饮食的第一步。

杰克：我同意。我觉得如今很多加工食品取代了传统的新鲜农产品，因此，也难怪现在很多年轻人患上了以前老年人才患的病。

凯特：是的，比如说糖尿病，现在患此病的青少年比以前多了很多，这是由于吃了过多的快餐引起的。

杰克：这很奇怪，不是吗？一方面，我们的生活里充斥着各种令人眼花缭乱的食品信息和最新的健身器材，但另一方面我们又被鼓励去追求休闲、充实的生活。

凯特：说得对。你知道，关于食物以及我们如何栽培、加工和食用的问题，多年来备受争议。

杰克：如果你问我的观点，我认为世界的迅速城市化、新鲜农产品生产成本的提高，还有家庭预算的减少和生活方式的改变，使得为越来越多的人口提供更便宜且更易制作的食物的竞争越来越激烈。

凯特：那么，你认为城市化的进程、食品成本的提高、家庭预算的缩减和生活方式的改变就是我们健康变差的罪魁祸首，是吗？

杰克：那样说过于简单化了。所有这些因素都改变了我们的饮食习惯，这就是我想要说的。

凯特：好吧，所以简单地说，我们已经放弃了传统的饮食习惯，完全接受了靠微波炉速成的饭菜。

杰克：也不全是。但是在某些方面，我们的饮食比二三十年前的好多了。

凯特：喝的方面怎么样？我们应该喝些什么？

杰克：至于喝的方面，没有什么比得过喝大量的水了。它能够帮助我们恢复体力，还有冷却、清洁和提供营养的作用。

凯特：有人说，水是万灵药。

杰克：我不会说得那么绝对，但毫无疑问我们不能没有水。

凯特：我想起来了，对身体有益的饮料还包括茶，尤其是绿茶、花茶和普洱茶。

杰克：完全正确！也许有些人认为喝茶不够时尚，但我坚信茶有药用和医用价值。我可以凭经验告诉你，每天喝茶对我有什么好处。即使你认为它不起任何作用，你也可以放心，它对你绝对无害。

凯特：哇，这次谈话确实非常生动，也富有启发意义。

🎒 跨文化交际小常识

在喜欢谈论天气的西方国家中，英国人的这一喜好表现得尤为明显。这不仅是因为他们更讲究传统的绅士文化，还因为这与他们国家变幻莫测的天气特点有关。英国地处大西洋彼岸的西风带，是世界上少有的几个天气异常多变的国家之一。在英国，有时上午还是阳光普照，下午就会大雨淋漓，甚至一小时前还是晴空万里，一小时后就会雾气蒙蒙。因此，谈论或预测天气很自然地就成了英国人最经常的话题。但是，从人际交往的角度来看，谈论天气也不是绝对安全的，因为你可能喜欢艳阳高照，但别人可能喜欢的是阴雨连绵。所以，在谈论天气时，一定要注意方式，最好是只客观地描述，而不要加以评论。

Unit 4

Great Minds
伟大的思想家

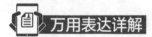 万用表达一览

- [ ] **came up for conversation** 提到了
- [ ] **heard of** 听说
- [ ] **look up** 查阅，查找

万用表达详解

1. came up for conversation

释 be mentioned 提到了

例 Zhu Zaiyu came up for conversation in music class today. He was the first to discover a mathematical solution for the equal-ratio chromatic scale.

今天音乐课上提到了朱载堉，他是第一个发现"十二平均律"的人。

2. heard of

释 If you have heard of someone or something, you know that that person or thing exists. 听说。

例 It's a tiny country that most people have never even heard of.

那是一个很小的国家，大多数人都没听说过。

3. look up

释 find sth. out by looking in sth. such as reference book or a list. 查阅，查找

例 I looked your address up in the personnel file.

我从人事档案里查到了你的地址。

 **实用对话场景**

Linda: We were talking about great minds in class today. Really fascinating stuff!

Mike: Who **came up for conversation**?

Linda: Well, Leonardo da Vinci of course, and some guy I had never **heard of** before.

Mike: Who was that?

Linda: Some guy was called Luca Pacioli, who taught Leonardo geometry.

Mike: Yes. He is a famous geometer and is also called the Father of Accounting.

Linda: Really? Did he invent accounting or something?

Mike: No. Accounting has been around for thousands of years, but he was the first to publish a book on the accounting practices of the Genoan and Venetian merchants, which we call the double-entry book-keeping method.

Linda: Naturally, we also talked about the great philosophers like Plato and Aristotle, but it all went in one ear and out the other.

Mike: Well, you can thank Plato and Aristotle for asking and answering many of life's important questions, and of course for teaching us their thinking techniques.

Linda: Thanks for the summary. I think I'll **look up** those two guys again.

Mike: Hey, glad I could help.

琳达：今天我们在课上讨论伟大的思想家，真的很有意思！

迈克：谈到了谁？

琳达：嗯，当然有达·芬奇，还有一个我以前没听说过的人。

迈克：是谁？

琳达：一个叫卢卡·帕乔利的人，他教过达·芬奇几何。

迈克：对。他是一位著名的几何学家，也被称为"会计学之父"。

琳达：真的吗？他发明了会计学还是怎样？

迈克：不是，会计学已有几千年了，但他是发表关于热那亚和威尼斯商人会计实务书的第一人，那种会计实务我们称为"复式记账法"。

琳达：我们自然也谈到了伟大的哲学家，像柏拉图和亚里士多德，但都是左耳进右耳出的。

迈克：嗯，你要谢谢柏拉图和亚里士多德提出并回答了很多人生的重要课题，当然还要谢谢他们教给我们思维的技巧。

琳达：谢谢你的总结，我想我要重新查阅他们两个人的资料。

迈克：嘿，很高兴我能帮上忙。

📠 跨文化交际小常识

　　工业革命以前，欧洲的上流社会、贵族世家的女孩子在成年以前，基本上是没有机会接触到异性的。但是到了一定的年纪，她们就要穿上礼服、盛装打扮，参加成人礼舞会，这标志着她们正式进入上流社会的社交圈。那个时候，社交的意义远不像现在这样广泛，女孩子进入社交圈的唯一目的就是物色一个门当户对的如意郎君。工业革命以后，中产阶级在经济上的地位逐渐上升，很多中产阶级的家长为了拥有特权，在自己的女儿成年后，也把她们送到各种社交舞会，以期望和贵族攀上亲戚，加入贵族的行列，取得政治上的地位。如今，这种具有特殊意义的社交舞会仍然不时地在国外贵族圈里上演。

Section 2 Intermediate 中级进阶

万用表达一览

☐ **stand the test of time** 经受了时间的考验

☐ **credit where credit is due** 给予应得的荣誉，该承认的还得承认，
实至名归

☐ **Now hang on just a sec!/Now hang on just a second!** 现在先等
一等!

☐ **One thing's for sure** 可以确定的是；有一样是肯定的

☐ **to this day** 直到今天

☐ **We can argue about... till the cows come home.** 我们可以一直讨
论 / 争论下去。

☐ **It doesn't change the fact** 这不能改变事实

☐ **something we can agree on** 我们在某些方面达成一致意见

万用表达详解

1. **stand the test of time**

   释 sth. maintains its usefulness/validity over a long period of
   time, despite attempts to discredit/disprove it 经受了时间的
   考验

   例 This type of construction has stood the test of time.
   这种建筑已经经受了时间的考验。

2. **credit where credit is due**

   释 acknowledge someone for a contribution where it is called
   for 给予应得的荣誉，该承认的还得承认，实至名归

   例 He was the one who first came up with the idea, so we should
   all give credit where credit is due.
   他是第一个提出这个主意的人，所以该承认的我们都得承认。

3. **Now hang on just a sec!/Now hang on just a second!**

   释 Used to express during a heated discussion to let someone know that they are making a mistake/Now wait just a minute! 现在先等一等。

   例 A: The word apple has always meant apple.

   "apple" 这个词的意思一直是苹果。

   B: Now hang on just a sec! That's not quite right. The old English word "appel" meant any kind of fruit.

   先等等！那不太对。在古英语里"appel"指的是任何一种水果。

4. **One thing's for sure**

   释 One thing is certain/What is certain is this 可以确定的是；有一样是肯定的

   例 A: The cashier tried to pull a fast one on me! Luckily I counted my change and found a fake note.

   这个收银员想揩我油水！幸好我数了一下零钱，发现了一张假币。

   B: What did you do?

   你是怎么做的？

   A: I refused to accept it and got my way. One thing's for sure, though. I'll never go shopping there again!

   我拒收啊，而且成功了，我以后肯定不会再去那儿买东西了！

5. **to this day**

   释 up until this day 直到今天

   例 To this day, I don't know how he did it.

   到今天我都不知道他是怎么做到的。

6. **We can argue about...till the cows come home.**

   释 We can argue about this forever. 我们可以一直讨论 / 争论下去。

   例 Who invented what and when first is still up for debate. We can argue about it till the cows come home.

谁发明了什么，什么时候发明的，还没有定论，我们可以一直讨论下去。

7. It doesn't change the fact

释 It doesn't alter the state of affairs/It makes no difference 这不能改变事实

例 Just because you did him a favor, which doesn't change the fact that you still owe him the money.

你帮了他一个忙，并不能改变你欠他钱这一事实。

8. something we can agree on

释 something we have no dispute with/no difference of opinion on 我们在某些方面达成一致意见

例 A: Finally! You agree there's no difference in our results, only in our methods.

你终于同意我们的结果没有不同，只是方法不同而已！

B: Yes.

是的。

A: Well, that's something we can agree on.

嗯，这一点我们都同意。

实用对话场景

Linda: I was just reading something about Isaac Newton. You know, we always talk of Einstein as being great, but Newton is far greater.

Mike: How so?

Linda: He really had brilliant, independent insights on gravity that have **stood the test of time**. Einstein, on the other hand, just tinkered with Newton's ideas about gravity for eight years.

Mike: But **credit where credit is due!** Einstein's insight was that gravity bends light.

Linda: True. But Newton discovered calculus.

Mike: ***Now hang on just a sec!*** Newton and Leibnitz both discovered calculus. The question is whether Leibnitz borrowed his ideas from Newton. I mean, they wrote to each other about mathematics. ***One thing's for sure,*** though. We use Leibnitz' calculus notation ***to this day.***

Linda: Well, ***we can argue about*** Newton's greatness ***till the cows come home. It doesn't change the fact*** that he was a great scientist.

Mike: So what about scientists today? Who are the great minds of today, do you think?

Linda: Stephen Hawking. No question about it.

Mike: Finally, ***something we can agree on!***

琳达：我在读一些关于艾萨克·牛顿的资料。你知道我们总是说爱因斯坦伟大，但牛顿更伟大。

迈克：怎么个伟大法？

琳达：他在万有引力方面的确有杰出的、独立的并且经受住时间考验的见解。而爱因斯坦在长达八年的时间里只是修改了牛顿在万有引力方面的理论。

迈克：但该承认的还得承认！爱因斯坦的远见在于（他发现了）万有引力会使光线弯曲。

琳达：对，但牛顿发明了微积分。

迈克：先等一等！牛顿和莱布尼茨两人发明了微积分，问题在于莱布尼茨是不是借用了牛顿的理论。我的意思是，他们互相给对方写信讨论数学。不过有一样是确定的，就是我们直到今天还在用莱布尼茨的微积分符号。

琳达：好吧，我们可以无休止地争论牛顿到底伟大在什么地方，反正也改变不了他是个伟大的科学家这一事实。

迈克：那今天的科学家怎么样？你觉得今天有哪些伟人？

琳达：毫无疑问，史蒂芬·霍金。

迈克：终于我们在某些地方达成一致了！

跨文化交际小常识

　　成人礼是在少男少女年龄满18岁时举行的象征迈向成人阶段的仪式。在成人礼上，通常都要进行成年宣誓（take an oath to adulthood）。其实，在中国也有成人礼。中国的成人礼已有长达数千年的历史，只不过在最近半个世纪很少举行。在中国，先秦时期的人们会为青年男子举行冠礼（capping ceremony），即加冠礼。随着现代社会的不断发展，人们的生活节奏也随之加快，加冠之礼正被人们慢慢遗弃，取而代之的是逐渐兴起的新时代成人礼，比如穿汉服（to wear traditional Han costumes）或祭拜孔子（to consecrate Confucius）等。

读书笔记

Section 3 Advanced 高级飞跃

万用表达一览

- ☐ **It's curious that in this day and age** 令人费解的是，当下……
- ☐ **in our own time** 我们这个时代
- ☐ **One exception would be...** 也许……是个例外
- ☐ **a genius in/at** 在……方面（领域）的天才
- ☐ **stand out** 脱颖而出
- ☐ **immune to** 不会影响，对……抗拒，对……免疫
- ☐ **skeptical of** 持怀疑态度的
- ☐ **so-called** 所谓的
- ☐ **in turn** 转而，相反
- ☐ **tackle thorny issues** 攻克棘手问题
- ☐ **make stunning breakthroughs** 做出突出贡献
- ☐ **overturn conventional wisdom** 颠覆人们传统的智慧
- ☐ **ways of approaching things** 处理问题的方式，做事的方式
- ☐ **wrap their brains around the most arcane or complex issues** 致力于最为神秘或复杂的课题
- ☐ **thoroughly disagreeable** 非常令人不快的
- ☐ **continue to inspire us** 不断地激励我们

万用表达详解

1. **It's curious that in this day and age**

    释 It's strange that in today's world 令人费解的是，当下……

    例 It's curious that in this day and age, we still have so much ignorance and poverty in the world.

    令人费解的是，当下世界还有那么多无知与贫困。

2. **in our own time**

   释 in this day and age/modern era 我们这个时代

   例 It seems to be a rare thing to find geniuses in our own time.

   在我们这个时代，发现天才似乎是很难的。

3. **One exception would be...**

   释 a case that is not subject to the rules 也许……是个例外

   例 One exception to the rule would be leaving work in case of a real emergency.

   只有一种情况例外，就是遇到紧急情况可以提前下班。

4. **a genius in/at**

   释 brilliant at/very skilled at/extremely shrewd in terms of 在……方面（领域）的天才

   例 Andy Warhol was a genius at picking his subjects. They were real icons of their day.

   安迪·霍沃非常擅长挑选绘画对象，这些绘画里的人物都是那个时代的偶像。

5. **stand out**

   释 very noticeable/very obvious 脱颖而出

   例 He stands out like a sore thumb.

   他很格格不入。

6. **immune to**

   释 resistant to/not bother 不会影响，对……抗拒，对……免疫

   例 I'm immune to his rude behavior. You know what they say "Sticks and stones may break my bones, but words will never hurt me"!

   我对他鲁莽的行为不予理睬。你知道有句俗话，"棍棒和石头也许会打断我的骨头，但话语却伤不了我！"

7. **skeptical of**

   释 have doubts about 持怀疑态度的

例 I can tell she's skeptical of what I'm saying. She rolled her eyes at me.

她对我翻了翻眼，我知道她对我所说的话持怀疑态度。

8. **so-called**

释 popularly known as 所谓的

例 All these so-called late bloomers are really just a little lost.

这些所谓的大器晚成的人，真的只是有点儿迷惘而已。

9. **in turn**

释 following that 转而，相反

例 Despite her hardships, she persevered. In turn, others began to see her as a shining example.

尽管遇到困难，但她坚持了下来，其他人因此将她视为榜样。

10. **tackle thorny issues**

释 take on/grapple with difficult/sensitive/delicate/tricky issues/problems 攻克棘手问题

例 At least he's not afraid to tackle thorny issues.

至少，遇到棘手的问题，他从不畏惧。

11. **make stunning breakthroughs**

释 make amazing/incredible advances 做出突出贡献

例 Scientists have made stunning breakthroughs in genetics.

科学家们在遗传学方面做出了突出的贡献。

12. **overturn conventional wisdom**

释 turn what is commonly accepted for a long time on its head 颠覆人们传统的智慧

例 You just can't leave well enough alone, can you? Why do you have to go and overturn centuries of conventional wisdom?

你就不能安于现状吗？为什么非得颠覆几个世纪以来的传统呢？

13. **ways of approaching things**

释 ways of going about doing sth. 处理问题的方式，做事的方式

例 He has a novel way of approaching these kinds of things.

他用一个新颖的方式来解决这些问题。

14. wrap their brains around the most arcane or complex issues

释 get one's head around sth. difficult and not commonly known or understood/try to figure out something that is complex and not commonly known or understood 致力于最为神秘或复杂的课题

例 I just can't wrap my brain around this formula. It doesn't make sense to me.

我就是无法理解这个方程式，我觉得讲不通啊。

15. thoroughly disagreeable

释 very objectionable 非常令人不快的

例 He's a thoroughly disagreeable person. I don't care how smart he is.

他是个一点都不讨人喜欢的人，我才不管他聪不聪明呢。

16. continue to inspire us

释 keep giving us ideas 不断地激励我们

例 Those novels continue to inspire me, no matter how often I read them.

不管我读多少遍，这些小说都一直激励着我。

实用对话场景

Linda: When I think of great minds, I immediately think of Shakespeare, Newton, Goethe, Michelangelo, Leonardo da Vinci and so on.

Mike: It's **curious that in this day and age**, we can seldom think of great minds **in our own time.**

Linda: **One exception would be** Stephen Hawking. He's considered **a genius in** the field of physics, because of his enormous contributions to quantum physics and the study of the universe.

Mike: You're right. Actually to be fair, brilliant minds are all around us. But I think that because of competing media and entertainment forms, as well as diverse interests among people, very few of these great minds **stand out**.

Linda: You have a point there. To be considered a great mind in today's world requires something special, because we've become so **immune to** the word "genius".

Mike: I'd also say that many people have become **skeptical of** the word "genius", since it was **so-called** 'geniuses', who devised very risky strategies for Wall Street to maximize profits. This **in turn** led to the Great Crash of 2008, and has preoccupied us ever since. So I'm sure, you can understand someone's reluctance these days to call anyone a genius.

Linda: But there are exceptions. We think of great minds who **tackle thorny issues**, like the global climate, and scientists who **make stunning breakthroughs** in medicine and health.

Mike: Right. Great minds typically **overturn conventional wisdom** or find innovative **ways of approaching things.**

Linda: They can **wrap their brains around the most arcane or complex issues** and make them comprehensible to us.

Mike: But not all great minds are likeable people. They can be **thoroughly disagreeable** too.

Linda: True.

Mike: But their life's work **continues to inspire us**. That's why they're geniuses.

Linda: I really enjoyed this chat. I'm looking forward to our next topic.

琳达：一想起伟大的思想家，莎士比亚、牛顿、歌德、米开朗琪罗及达·芬奇的名字便会立刻跃进我的脑海里。

迈克：令人费解的是，在当下找出属于这个时代的伟大的思想家却是一件很难的事情。

琳达：也许史蒂芬·霍金是个例外，他在量子物理学领域和宇宙研究方面做出了突出的贡献，是人们公认的物理学天才。

迈克：你说得对。在我看来，我们身边其实不乏天才学者，但身处追求享乐和争名夺利的社会，只有少数伟大的思想家能脱颖而出。

琳达：你说得挺有道理。再加上当今这个时代人们对"天才"这个词语又具有相当的免疫力，因此想要在这个时代成为伟大的思想家就必须具备某些特质。

迈克：我也同意，很多人对于"天才"这个词已是满腹狐疑，因为正是那些所谓"天才"的人，不择手段地在华尔街让自己赚得盆钵满盈，导致了 2008 年次贷危机，并成了我们生活中的头等大事。我想你一定能够理解为何现在有些人不屑于称呼任何一个人为天才了。

琳达：但我们也不能够一概而论，那些研究全球气候变暖等棘手问题，以及在医疗健康领域做出突出贡献的科学家们仍然是伟大的思想家。

迈克：是的，伟大的思想家往往会颠覆人们传统的智慧，或者寻找创新的方式来解决问题。

琳达：他们能全方位地掌握最为神秘或者复杂的课题，并将它们变得通俗易懂。

迈克：然而并非所有的思想家都是讨人喜欢的，他们可能也会让人感到非常厌恶。

琳达：对。

迈克：但是他们毕生的工作不断地激励着我们，这就是为什么他们成为天才的原因。

琳达：我真的很喜欢这次的聊天，我期待着下一个话题。

跨文化交际小常识

颜色在中西方不同文化背景下也被赋予不同的含义。例如，红色在中国是喜庆幸福的色彩，结婚典礼、开业典礼等重大场合都是用红色作为点缀，大红灯笼、大红对联、大红嫁衣、大红中国结都是中国的传统代表物件。但红色在西方文化中具有贬义色彩，相关的词汇red assed（火冒三丈的），in the red（财政赤字的），red hands（刽子手），red headed（狂怒的），red flag（危险信号）等，他们都联系着血腥、暴怒、残酷、危险等恶劣事件。

读书笔记

Unit 5 | Maturing
成熟

Section 1 Basic 初级基础

万用表达一览

☐ **You don't know what it's like...** 你都不知道……是怎么样的

☐ **Try me!** 试试看！来试试我吧！

☐ **rough** 艰苦，恶劣

☐ **go through** 遭受，经历

☐ **get even tougher** 变得更难

☐ **done with** 完毕，毕业后

☐ **free as** 自由得像……

☐ **I've been there!** 我也曾经跟你一样！

☐ **What do you say?** 你怎么说？

万用表达详解

1. **You don't know what it's like...**

   释 You don't understand the situation... 你都不知道……是怎么样的

   例 You don't know what it's like in these dorms in summer. The mosquitoes are a nightmare.

   你无法想象夏天时这些宿舍是什么样子的，蚊子多得像噩梦一样。

2. **Try me!**

   释 Give me a chance! (to show you what I know)/Test me! 试试看！来试试我吧！

例 A: I don't think you could possibly understand me.

我觉得你不可能懂我。

B: Try me!

试试看!

3. **rough**

释 difficult 艰苦,恶劣

例 The weather is going to be rough for the next few weeks. Get used to it!

接下来的几个星期,天气会变得很恶劣。习惯一下吧!

4. **go through**

释 experience (difficulty/hardship) 遭受,经历

例 We have to go through some pain, whether we like it or not. That's just a fact of life.

无论我们喜欢与否,我们都必须经历一些痛苦,那就是人生。

5. **get even tougher**

释 get even more difficult 变得更难

例 Mark my words! The exams will get even tougher next year.

记住我的话!明年的考试会更难。

6. **done with**

释 finished with 完毕,毕业后

例 When he was done with school, he went on to a successful career in electrical engineering.

他从学校毕业以后,成功地踏上了电机工程的职业之路。

7. **free as**

释 as free as 自由得像……

例 A: How do you feel?

你感觉怎么样?

B: I feel free as a bird. No responsibilities, and only my studies to think about. It can't get much better than this.

我感觉自由得像只小鸟，只管学习，不需考虑责任，没有什么比这更好了。

8. I've been there!

释 I've been in your shoes,/I've experienced what you are experiencing now. 我也曾经跟你一样！

例 I've been there, done that!
我曾经也那样做过！

9. What do you say?

释 How about it?/What do you think? 你怎么说？

例 How about we go for a drive in the countryside? What do you say?
我们开车去乡村兜风怎样？你怎么说？

 **实用对话场景**

Jenny: ***You don't know what it's like*** in school.

Tom: ***Try me***!

Jenny: The same boring lessons day after day and the same routines year after year.

Tom: Growing up is ***rough***. We all have to ***go through*** it. And once you're an adult, it ***gets even tougher***.

Jenny: No way! When I'm ***done with*** school, I'll be ***free as*** a bird!

Tom: Well, birds have to eat and forage for food too. You don't realize it now, but school is such a short period of time in your life. Make use of it because you won't get it back.

Jenny: What do you think I should do?

Tom: Put on a happy face tomorrow and start liking school, even if you don't. It works. Trust me! ***I've been there!*** So ***what do you say?***

Jenny: Good idea. I do feel better now. Thanks.

珍妮：你都想象不到校园生活是怎么样的。

汤姆：说来听听！

珍妮：日复一日，年复一年，上无聊的课，做一样的事。

汤姆：成长是个艰难的过程，我们都必须经历这些，一旦你长大成人，生活会变得更艰难。

珍妮：才不是！当我完成学业时，我就会像只小鸟一样自由！

汤姆：嗯，鸟也要吃东西，要觅食。你现在体会不到，但学校只是你生命中很短的一段时间。好好利用它吧，因为这是你找不回来的。

珍妮：你觉得我应该做些什么？

汤姆：明天把笑容挂在脸上，开始喜欢学校，即使你不喜欢。那很有效，相信我吧！我以前也上过学！你怎么说？

珍妮：好主意，我现在感觉好多了。谢谢。

跨文化交际小常识

在中国传统社会里，邻里关系可以说是最基本、最重要的人际关系。如今，在市场经济这一巨大浪潮的冲击下，人们对邻里交往的依赖性逐渐减弱。其实，这一现象在西方社会也很普遍。如何在维护各自家庭相对独立的同时，又融洽邻里关系，是一个亟待解决的问题。在许多西方国家的中产阶级聚居地，人们通常举办"邻里派对"（neighborhood party）来维护和加强邻里关系。一般来说，派对是由社区的热心居民发起，除了张贴公告之外，还给每家每户发送邀请信，告知派对的时间、地点、活动内容以及其他注意事项等，以便大家早做准备。

Section 2 Intermediate 中级进阶

万用表达一览

☐ **What came up?** 提到了什么？

☐ **have dreams of** 希望做，梦想做

☐ **have no idea** 什么也不知道，搞不清楚，毫无头绪

☐ **haven't a clue** 完全不知道

☐ **at that age** 在那个年纪

☐ **No matter what I do, it's never enough.** 无论我做什么，还是不够！

☐ **It feels like...** 感觉像……

万用表达详解

1. **What came up?**

   释 What topics were discussed? 提到了什么？

   例 A: What came up in the math test?

   数学测验考了什么？

   B: Calculus for one thing.

   主要考了微积分。

2. **have dreams of**

   释 dream of doing 希望做，梦想做

   例 Everyone has dreams of stardom at that age.

   那个年龄段的人都希望成为明星。

3. **have no idea**

   释 not have a clue/really not know 什么也不知道，搞不清楚，毫无头绪

   例 I have no idea what I want to do with my life.

   我不知道自己想过怎样的生活。

4. **haven't a clue**

   释 have no idea/really not know 完全不知道

   例 I haven't a clue what the next step is.

   我完全不知道下一步要怎么做。

5. **at that age**

   释 at the age (in question) 在那个年纪

   例 At that age, he didn't know what he wanted to be. It only came to him later on.

   在那个年纪的时候,他不知道自己想做什么,之后他才知道答案。

6. **No matter what I do, it's never enough.**

   释 It makes no difference what I do. It's not enough/It's inadequate... 无论我做什么，还是不够！

   例 A: No matter what I do, it's never enough! I just keep plugging away at English, but I'm still no further ahead.

   无论我做什么，还是不够！我一直孜孜不倦地学英语，但一直没什么进步。

   B: You've got to be kidding me! You made it this far. Something must have stuck.

   你在跟我说笑吧！你已经学了一段时间了,肯定学到些东西的。

7. **It feels like...**

   释 I have the feeling that 感觉像……

   例 It feels like I've just run a marathon!

   我感觉像是刚跑完马拉松!

实用对话场景

Jenny: We were talking about our future in class today.

Tom: And? ***What came up?***

Jenny: Well, a lot of people ***have dreams of*** going abroad to study, and some people ***have no idea*** what they want to do.

Tom: Well, that's normal. Most people **haven't a clue** about anything when they're teenagers. They know what they need for school but not for life. There are just too many distractions **at that age**.

Jenny: You took the words right out of my mouth!

Tom: That's because I've been there.

Jenny: On the one hand, I'm having a great time in school, but on the other hand I feel all this pressure. **No matter what I do**, it's **never enough. It feels like** a rat race.

Tom: That's because it is. And life doesn't get easier, but it does get more interesting.

Jenny: I can't wait!

珍妮：今天我们在课堂上讨论了我们的未来。

汤姆：你们提到了什么？

珍妮：很多人有出国留学的愿望，也有一些人不知道自己将来做什么。

汤姆：嗯，那很正常。很多人在青少年时期对任何事情都没什么想法。他们知道要怎么上学，却不知道要怎么生活。那个年龄段的人有太多让自己分心的事情了。

珍妮：你说出了我想说的话！

汤姆：那是因为我是过来人。

珍妮：一方面，我在学校度过了很愉快的时光，但另一方面，我感觉到了各种各样的压力。无论我做什么，感觉永远都不够，就好像这是一场激烈的竞争一样。

汤姆：那是因为它就是激烈的竞争。而且生活不会变得容易，但会变得更有趣。

珍妮：我等不及了！

跨文化交际小常识

公共洗衣房（**public laundry room**）在中国可能还是一个新鲜事物，但在美国，相当一部分人一辈子都不会考虑买房子，不买房子就只能租公寓，而绝大部分公寓房是空房出租，需要租户自带家具电器。所以，为了尽量减少日后搬家的麻烦，美国相当一部分人，特别是喜欢迁徙的年轻人一般都不会买洗衣机和干衣机，他们通常会积攒一个礼拜的脏衣服拿去洗衣房清洗并烘干，简单方便，经济实惠。一家运作良好的洗衣房永远是干净整洁，充满阳光的，摆放着舒适的桌椅，整个洗衣房里洋溢着洗涤剂的清香。

读书笔记

Section 3 Advanced 高级飞跃

万用表达一览

☐ **deem to be** 认为

☐ **countless stories** 很多的故事，数不清的故事

☐ **look forward to** 期待着

☐ **Ask any...** 问任何人

☐ **I'd give anything/I'd give my eye teeth** 我愿意付出一切

☐ **that come with** 随……而来

☐ **You see what I mean?** 现在你明白我的意思吗？

☐ **upsides and downsides/upsides as well as downsides** 优点和缺点

☐ **Only time will tell...** 时间会证明……

万用表达详解

1. **deem to be**

   释 regard as 认为

   例 She was deemed to be too young to participate in the match.
   大家认为她年纪太小，不适合参加比赛。

2. **countless stories**

   释 too many stories to count 很多的故事，数不清的故事

   例 I have heard countless stories about the haunted house, but I don't believe a word of them and neither should you.
   我听到过许多关于这间鬼屋的故事，但我不相信，你也不应该相信。

3. **look forward to**

   释 await with pleasure 期待着

   例 A: I look forward to the rematch. My team lost because they had an off-day.

我期待复赛，我们队输了是因为那天很倒霉。

B: Who're you kidding? I watched the match too. My team won because they played better than your team. A rematch is just going to confirm that.

你在跟谁开玩笑呢？我也看了比赛，我们队获胜是因为我们的队员比你们的打得好。复赛就会证明这一点的。

4. **Ask any...**

释 question anybody 问任何人

例 Ask anyone about me. They'll confirm everything I'm saying.

随便问哪个人关于我的事情，他们都会证实我所说的一切。

5. **I'd give anything/I'd give my eye teeth**

释 I would do anything 我愿意付出一切

例 I'd give anything to be back in school.

为了能重返校园，我愿意付出一切。

6. **that come with**

释 come together with 随……而来

例 I like the perks that come with the job.

我喜欢这份工作享有的特别待遇。

7. **You see what I mean?**

释 Do you understand what I'm saying? 现在你明白我的意思吗？

例 You see what I mean? You take your eyes off the kids for one second and the house is destroyed!

现在你明白我的意思了吧？你只要一分钟不看着那些孩子，屋子就会乱成一团糟！

8. **upsides and downsides/upsides as well as downsides**

释 benefits and drawbacks/advantages and disadvantages 优点和缺点

例 Settling in here has its upsides and downsides. But I like to focus on the upsides.

在这里定居有利也有弊，但我喜欢把注意力放在它的优点上。

9. **Only time will tell...**

释 We will know after some time... 时间会证明……

例 A: Do you think it was wise moving here?

你觉得搬来这儿明智吗？

B: Only time will tell.

时间会告诉你一切的。

实用对话场景

Jenny: When I think of the word "maturing" I think of getting older. We're all maturing day by day.

Tom: Right. Some people mature faster than others.

Jenny: Maturing can be both physical and mental.

Tom: Good point. Most people use the word to refer to someone's mental age. If you're a teenager, it's OK to like certain things, but as soon as you become a legal adult, you're expected to conform to what society *deems to be* appropriate adult behavior.

Jenny: Maturing is difficult, even for adults.

Tom: I know what you mean. We want to be young forever. It's a natural desire. There are *countless stories* in history and folklore of finding an elixir for eternal youth .

Jenny: Right. It's an age-old dream to stay young forever. The reality is that we all *look forward to* growing up, but don't necessarily like the physical aging that comes with it. *Ask any* athlete or celebrity what they think of aging.

Tom: They'd probably say something like, "*I'd give anything* to be young again".

Jenny: But others like the responsibilities and lifestyle *that come with* age. When you're 19, no one would give you the responsibilities of a 30 year-old. No one would ever think of you as mature enough. ***You see what I mean?***

Tom: I think so. Maturing has its ***upsides as well as its downsides***. ***Only time will tell*** what they are.

Jenny: You could put it that way. Yes.

珍妮：当我想到"成熟"这个词的时候，我想到年龄越来越大，我们都日渐成熟。

汤姆：是的，有些人比其他人成熟得快些。

珍妮：成熟包括生理上的成熟和心理上的成熟。

汤姆：说得好。大多数人会用这个词去谈论人的心理年龄。如果你还是个青少年，那你喜欢做某些事情是没问题的。但是如果你已经从青少年成长为法律意义上的成年人，那么大多数人就会认为，你的行为举止应该符合成年人的标准。

珍妮：即使对于成年人来说，想要在处事上表现成熟，也不是一件易事。

汤姆：我明白你的意思。我们希望永远年轻，这是人的本性。历史和民间传说中，有很多关于人们寻找灵丹妙药以保长生不老的故事。

珍妮：是的，长生不老是古今人类的梦想。在现实中，我们都期待着长大，但不一定喜欢随着年龄增长而带来的生理上的老化。你可以问问任何一名运动员或名人他们对变老的看法。

汤姆：他们很可能会这样告诉你："我愿付出一切，只为再次变年轻。"

珍妮：但是也有人喜欢随着年龄而来的责任感和生活方式的改变。当你十九岁时，没有人会给你三十岁的人才承担的责任，没有人会认为你成熟到足够担当起那样一份责任。你明白我的意思吗？

汤姆：我想我明白。成熟有优点，也有缺点，只有时间才能告诉我们到底这些优点和缺点是什么。

珍妮：是的，你可以这样解释。

跨文化交际小常识

　　诚信是美国人的基本准则之一。美国人对于诚信的狂热追求，可以体现在他们的超市购物上。在很多大型超市，结账方式通常有两种：个人自主结账以及传统的收银员结账。很多大型超市都会24小时开放，晚上9点以后一般都会采用自主结账方式，即顾客自己刷条形码，自己付钱。一切都让顾客DIY，很考验个人诚信，因为即使你不付钱直接把东西拿走，被抓住的可能性也不是很大。使超市得以长久维持并坚持采用这个方式运营的根本前提就是每个消费者的诚信。

读书笔记

Unit 6

Friends & Enemies
朋友和敌人

Section 1　Basic 初级基础

万用表达一览

☐ **stormy** 暴风雨似的，猛烈的，多风波的

☐ **funnily enough** 有趣的是

☐ **Do you want to know something odd?** 你想知道奇怪的是什么

吗？/ 你想知道一些奇怪的事吗？

万用表达详解

1. **stormy**

　　释 not calm 暴风雨似的，猛烈的，多风波的

　　例 They had a stormy relations.

　　　　他们的关系曾经时好时坏。

2. **funnily enough**

　　释 strangely enough 有趣的是

　　例 Funnily enough, we never met again after that.

　　　　有趣的是，从那以后我们再没见过面。

3. **Do you want to know something odd?**

　　释 Do you want to know a strange thing? 你想知道奇怪的是什么

　　　　吗？/ 你想知道一些奇怪的事吗？

　　例 Do you want to know something odd? I don't know what that

　　　　word means, but I hear it all the time.

　　　　你想知道奇怪的是什么吗？我总听到这个词，但我就是不知道

它是什么意思。

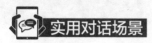 **实用对话场景**

Cindy: We were talking about famous friendships in class today.

Dale: Who did you talk about?

Cindy: Mostly about people who had ***stormy*** relations.

Dale: Such as?

Cindy: Thomas Jefferson and John Adams.

Dale: Yeah. They didn't like each other for years.

Cindy: But ***funnily enough***, in later years, they wrote to each other constantly.

Dale: ***Do you want to know something odd?***

Cindy: What?

Dale: They died on the same day and Adams's famous last words were: "Jefferson lives!"

辛迪：今天我们在课上讨论了伟大的友谊。

戴尔：你们谈到了谁?

辛迪：大多是那些关系时好时坏的人。

戴尔：比如说?

辛迪：汤姆斯·杰斐逊和约翰·亚当斯。

戴尔：嗯，他们不喜欢对方很多年。

辛迪：但有趣的是，他们在晚年经常给对方写信。

戴尔：你想知道一些奇怪的事么?

辛迪：什么事?

戴尔：他们俩同一天去世，而亚当斯的遗言是"杰斐逊万岁！"

跨文化交际小常识

1620年，著名的"五月花号（Ship Mayflower）"轮船满载不堪忍受英国国内宗教迫害的清教徒102人到达美洲。1620年和 1621年之交的冬天，他们遇到了难以想象的困难，处在饥寒交迫之中，冬天过去时，活下来的移民只有50多人。这时心地善良的印第安人给移民送来了生活必需品，还特地派人教他们怎样狩猎、捕鱼和种植玉米、南瓜。在印第安人的帮助下，移民们终于获得了丰收，在欢庆丰收的日子，按照宗教传统习俗，移民规定了感谢上帝的日子，并决定为感谢印第安人的真诚帮助，邀请他们一同庆祝节日。

读书笔记

Section 2 Intermediate 中级进阶

万用表达一览

☐ **I can't put it down.** 我爱不释手，我放不下。

☐ **The story is set...** 故事发生在……

☐ **fine balancing act** 脆弱的平衡关系（意思为：这种平衡比较微妙 /
脆弱，稍不留意就会造成失衡）

☐ **out to get each other** 攻击对方

☐ **face to face** 面对面

☐ **like a game of chess** 像棋赛博弈一样

☐ **How far into the novel are you?** 你看到哪儿了？

☐ **I'm about half way through it.** 我快看到一半了。

☐ **stand-off** 势均力敌

☐ **It's a battle of wits.** 那是一场智慧的较量。

万用表达详解

1. **I can't put it down.**

   释 I can't stop reading it. 我爱不释手，我放不下。

   例 This spy thriller is so good, I can't put it down.
   这部谍战片太好看了，我简直爱不释手。

2. **The story is set...**

   释 The story happens... 故事发生在……

   例 The story is set in a modern-day urban setting, somewhere in
   China.
   故事发生在今天中国的某个城市。

3. **fine balancing act**

   释 a delicate balancing act 脆弱的平衡关系（意思为：这种平衡

比较微妙 / 脆弱，稍不留意就会造成失衡）

例 Being a working mother these days is a fine balancing act.

如今做职业母亲很难把握家庭和工作之间的平衡。

4. **out to get each other**

释 trying to undermine/undercut one another/spoil things for each other 攻击对方

例 Those two were out to get each other from the get-go, so it doesn't surprise me they were fired.

他们俩从一开始就企图攻击对方，所以他们被炒鱿鱼，我并不感到惊讶。

5. **face to face**

释 in person/being in the presence of another 面对面

例 I still prefer face-to-face conversations to conversations over Skype or iChat.

相比用 Skype 或 iChat，我更喜欢面对面地聊天。

6. **like a game of chess**

释 just as in a game of chess 像棋赛博弈一样

例 He approaches his career like a game of chess. He's always one step ahead of his nearest rivals.

他把自己的职业生涯当成棋赛博弈来看待，他总是比紧追其后的对手快一步。

7. **How far into the novel are you?**

释 How much of the novel have you read? 你看到哪儿了？

例 A: I can't wait to borrow your novel. How far into the novel are you anyway?

我迫不及待地想要借你的小说，你看到哪儿了？

B: I'm on the last chapter.

我在看最后一章了。

8. **I'm about half way through it.**

释 I've read almost 50% of it. 我快看到一半了。

例 I'm about half-way through the movie right now.

这部电影我快看到一半了。

9. **stand-off**

释 neither side submits or yields any ground/neither side makes a move until the other side does 势均力敌

例 A: What's the situation right now?

现在情况怎么样?

B: It's a stand-off between the two armies. No side has the advantage right now.

两军势均力敌，现在两边都没什么优势。

10. **It's a battle of wits.**

释 Each side tries to outwit the other 那是一场智慧的较量。

例 It's a battle of wits. Only the shrewdest survive the course.

那是一场智慧的较量，只有最精明的人才能在这个过程中活下来。

实用对话场景

Cindy: I'm reading a novel right now and **I can't put it down.**

Dale: What's it about?

Cindy: **The story is set** on an island somewhere in the Pacific. There's a small population of islanders, and they're in a power struggle with each other.

Dale: What do they want?

Cindy: Control of the island. To assume power, they have to outwit each other, but need each other's help at the same time. It's a **fine balancing act**. Secretly everyone's **out to get each other**, but **face to face** they're best friends. It's all **like a game of chess**. There are no friends or enemies.

Dale: ***How far into the novel are you?***

Cindy: ***I'm about half way through it.*** It's a tense ***stand-off.*** No one knows who's a real friend or enemy. ***It's a battle of wits.***

Dale: Hey, when you're done with it, can I borrow it?

Cindy: You bet!

辛迪：我现在在读一本小说，简直爱不释手。

戴尔：是关于什么的？

辛迪：故事发生在太平洋的某个岛上。岛上有为数不多的岛民，他们相互之间有权利斗争。

戴尔：他们想要什么？

辛迪：想控制岛屿。为了得到权力，他们要相互斗智斗勇，但同时也需要相互帮助。这是一种权衡之举啊。暗地里每个人都企图攻击对方，但见面时他们都是最好的朋友，就像棋赛博弈一样。世上没有绝对的朋友，也没有绝对的敌人。

戴尔：这本小说你看到哪里了？

辛迪：我快看完一半了。真是势均力敌啊，没有人知道谁是真正的朋友，谁是真正的敌人，那真是一场智慧的较量。

戴尔：嘿，你看完后我可以借来看吗？

辛迪：当然！

跨文化交际小常识

　　在美国，折价券（coupon）的运用范围非常广泛，既可以在网上使用，也可以在商店里使用，其价值从几毛钱到上千元都有。折价券里罗列的商品也五花八门，不过大部分是食物类的，其他日常用品也比较多。如果你善于运用这种折价券，就可以省下一大笔钱。此外，在美国做生意几乎没有讲价的习惯，看好了你就买，想讲价，没门。所以，如果你拿着折价券去买东西，就等于变相地自已寻找好处。美国的"coupon"大致可以分为两种，一种是"厂家折价券"（manufacturer coupon），一种是"店铺折价券"（store coupon）。有时，这两种折价券是可以同时使用的，这也是最省钱的方式。

读书笔记

Section 3 Advanced 高级飞跃

万用表达一览

☐ **That's not to say you can't...** 这并不是说你不能……

☐ **happen to** 实际上，事实上

☐ **You know the old saying...** 你知道有句老话（谚语）……

☐ **I remember that line** 我记得一句台词

☐ **I tend to think** 我倾向于认为

☐ **Keep you "together".** 保持清醒！

☐ **no matter what** 不论什么，不管何事

☐ **Don't get me started!** 别和我提……，别逼我打开话匣子抱怨……

☐ **Let's just say...** 这样说吧，我们只能说

☐ **So why not...** 所以为什么不……

万用表达详解

1. **That's not to say you can't...**

   释 I'm not saying you can't ... 这并不是说你不能……

   例 I prefer not going out before an exam. That's not to say I shouldn't.

   我更喜欢考试前待在家里，这并不是说我不应该出门。

2. **happen to**

   释 actually/as a matter of fact 实际上，事实上

   例 I happen to eat porridge every morning.

   事实上，我每天早上都喝粥。

3. **You know the old saying...**

   释 You know the old proverb/statement... 你知道有句老话（谚语）……

例 You know the old saying "When the going gets tough, the tough get going".

你知道有句老话叫作"越挫越勇"。

4. I remember that line

释 I remember that quote (what the actor said in the movie) 我记得一句台词

例 I remember that line from *the Marx Brothers*. That's vintage comedy.

我记得《马克思兄弟》的一句台词。那是一部怀旧喜剧。

5. I tend to think

释 I'm inclined to think 我倾向于认为

例 I tend to think outside the box.

我善于创造性地思考。

6. Keep you "together".

释 Stay sane. Don't go crazy! 保持清醒！

例 Come on! Keep it together! You just had a bad day. It'll blow over. You'll see.

拜托！清醒点！你只是今天过得不好而已，你会看到一切都会好起来的。

7. no matter what

释 No matter what happens/It doesn't matter what happens. / Come what may/Come hell or high water/ 不论什么，不管何事

例 You're my friend, no matter what.

不管怎样，你都是我的朋友。

8. Don't get me started!

释 Don't let me start complaining. 别和我提……，别逼我打开话匣子抱怨……

例 Don't get me started on him! You know I don't like him.

别跟我提他！你知道我不喜欢他。

9. **Let's just say...**

释 Simply put/often used before expressing something delicately, not forcefully or crudely 这样说吧，我们只能说

例 It's complicated. Let's just say I know things that you don't know and leave it at that.

好复杂啊。这样说吧，我知道你不知道的事情，就到此为止吧。

10. **So why not...**

释 So, why don't you 所以为什么不……

例 You won't find a parking spot there. So why not just park the car here and walk the rest of the way?

在那儿你是找不到停车位的，所以为什么不把车停到这儿，然后走过去呢？

实用对话场景

Cindy: You want to know about friends and enemies? Friends and enemies are more or less like oil and water. They can never really mix. ***That's not to say you can't*** talk to your enemies. We ***happen to*** do that every day. ***You know the old saying*** "Keep your friends close but your enemies closer".

Dale: Yes. ***I remember that line*** from *The Godfather*. When I think of friends, though, ***I tend to think*** of people, whose views are ***somewhat similar to*** mine. That's not to say, they always coincide.

Cindy: Right. Friendships are built on similarities as well as differences. Isn't that so? But one thing's for sure. Friends ***keep you 'together'.***

Dale: You mean sane?

Cindy: Yes. Without friends the world would be a very lonely place.

Your true friends are loyal to you and stick up for you **no matter what.**

Dale: Then of course you have your 'fair-weather friends' who are – you guessed it – your best friends when times are good.

Cindy: Right. As soon as you find yourself in deep trouble, though, they show their true colors and run for the hills. What about your enemies?

Dale: Well, **don't get me started** on them. You'll know soon enough who they are. They don't like you for different reasons. It could be that they envy you for your talents or your personality.

Cindy: No one wants enemies of course, but the truth is that not everyone is going to like you as much as you like yourself. **Let's just say** we all have our ways. We all have our ideas of how the world should work, and we all feel that our friends are people who come closest to our idea of how our world should be.

Dale: Right. What's more, when our friends are around, everything's right with the world. When we see our enemies, though, we tend to become more defensive and wary.

Cindy: I suppose you could ignore them or try to make peace with them.

Dale: You could rise above them, outdo them, even forget about them.

Cindy: You could also learn from them.

Dale: Why learn from them?

Cindy: It's possible to learn from your enemies, too. **So why not** make them your "frenemies"?

Dale: Ha! Good one.

Cindy: I thought you'd like that.

辛迪：你想了解朋友与敌人吗？朋友与敌人或多或少像油和水，永远不可能相溶，但这并不代表你不能跟你的敌人进行对话。事实上我们每天都在和他们沟通。有句老话说："亲近你的朋友，但更要亲近你的敌人。"

戴尔：是的，我记得那是电影《教父》里的一句台词。谈到朋友，我想到那些观点和我比较相近的人们，但这些相近并不意味着我们完全一致。

辛迪：对，友谊不仅建立在相似点之上，而且还建立在差异之上，不是吗？但有一点可以肯定的是，朋友使你保持清醒。

戴尔：你的意思是头脑清醒，是吧？

辛迪：是的，没有朋友，世界将会变得十分寂寞。不论发生什么，你真正的朋友会忠于你并保护你。

戴尔：当然，也有"酒肉朋友"。你猜得到的，在你一帆风顺的时候，他们是你最好的伴。

辛迪：是的，不过，一旦你遇到困难，他们就会露出本来面目，跑得无影无踪。你的敌人又是怎么样的呢？

戴尔：唉，别跟我提他们了，你很快就会知道答案。他们因为种种原因不喜欢你，比如，他们嫉妒你的才华和个性。

辛迪：没有人希望自己有敌人，但事实是，不是每个人都会像你喜欢自己一样喜欢你。我们只能说，我们都有自己的做事方式，都有自己的世界观，而我们都觉得朋友就是那些有着和自己非常相近的世界观的人。

戴尔：是的。还有，朋友在身边时，我们觉得世界一切都是对的，但遇到敌人时，就会变得更小心警惕。

辛迪：我想你可以忽略他们或跟他们言归于好。

戴尔：你可以超越他们，胜过他们，甚至忘掉他们。

辛迪：你也可以向他们学习。

戴尔：为什么要向他们学习呢？

辛迪：你也是可以向你的敌人学习的，所以为什么不让他们成为你的"友敌"呢？

戴尔：哈哈，好主意！

辛迪：我想你也会喜欢的。

跨文化交际小常识

　　美国的医生主要分为两类，一类是专科医生（specialist），一类是私人医生（primary-care physician，PCP）。专科医生可以是全职在医院工作的，也可以自己在外面开私人专科诊所，例如，医院的妇产科、心脏科、皮肤科、诊断科等，或者单独的耳鼻喉专科诊所。私人医生一般称为家庭医生，其实并不是有钱人特有的消费项目，大多数低收入且有医疗保险的人群也都有自己的私人医生。PCP具体含义是"在一项医疗保险计划里最基本及主要服务提供者，如医生或医务专业人士"，也可称为"personal care physician"或"personal care provider"，一般都称为"初级保健医师"。他们有自己的诊所，包看百病，但是遇到自己解决不了的病患，就会把病人转到其他的专业科室去治疗。

读书笔记

Unit 7

Famous Detectives
著名的侦探

万用表达一览

- [ ] **Let me guess.** 让我猜猜。
- [ ] **You took the words right out of my mouth.** 你说了我想说的话。
- [ ] **the poor guy** 这可怜的家伙
- [ ] **A real shame!** 真遗憾！

万用表达详解

1. **Let me guess.**

   释 Let me predict what happens next. 让我猜猜。

   例 A: Gravity varies slightly with latitude. True or false?

   　　纬度不同，重力也略有不同，对不对？

   　　B: Let me guess! True!

   　　让我猜猜！对！

2. **You took the words right out of my mouth.**

   释 You said exactly what I was going to say. 你说了我想说的话。

   例 A: This duck is delicious. It's simply the best I've ever tasted!

   　　这鸭子真好吃，这简直是我尝过的最好吃的！

   　　B: You took the words right out of my mouth!

   　　你说了我想说的话！

3. **the poor guy**

   释 the unfortunate man 这可怜的家伙

例 The poor guy didn't stand a chance against them. He was outnumbered 10 to 1 (10:1).

这可怜的家伙没有任何机会战胜他们，他 10 比 1 大比分落后。

4. A real shame!

释 very/really unfortunate 真遗憾！

例 It's a real shame we can't meet more often.

我们不能经常见面，真遗憾。

 **实用对话场景**

Grace: What are you reading?

Frank: I'm reading a book on famous detectives.

Grace: You mean, like Sherlock Homes?

Frank: Well, actually, he's a fictional consulting detective. I'm talking about real ones. The first known private investigator (private detective) was a Frenchman, named Francois-Eugene Vidocq. He inspired many famous authors, like Charles Dickens, Arthur Conan Doyle, and Edgar Alan Poe. Another guy, called Allen Pinkerton, prevented President Abraham Lincoln's assassination, while he was on his way to his presidential inauguration. Lincoln later asked Pinkerton to create the Secret Service.

Grace: Tell me more about Pinkerton. He sounds really interesting.

Frank: All I know is that he was Scottish and left Scotland for America when he was 23. This was in the 1840s when rail transportation was becoming very popular.

Grace: Oh. **Let me guess.** There were lots of train robberies at that time as well.

Frank: **You took the words right out of my mouth.** So his detective agency solved many of these crimes. Eventually he met Abraham Lincoln.

Grace: So what happened to him?

Frank: Well, ***the poor guy*** slipped and fell, bit his tongue, and later died from the resulting infection.

Grace: Sad. Such a smart guy too.

Frank: Yeah. ***A real shame!***

格蕾丝：你在读什么？

弗兰克：我在读一本关于著名侦探的书。

格蕾丝：你指的是像夏洛克·福尔摩斯这样的人？

弗兰克：呃，事实上他是一个虚构的私家侦探，我说的是真实存在的侦探。第一个有名的私家侦探是一个叫弗朗斯科·尤根·维多克的法国人，他给很多像查尔斯·狄更斯、阿瑟·柯南道尔、埃德加·艾伦·坡这样著名作家以灵感。另一个人叫艾伦·平克顿，他在林肯前往总统就职演讲的路上阻止了对其进行的刺杀行动，之后林肯总统要求平克顿设立特工处。

格蕾丝：多告诉我一点平克顿的事情吧，他听起来很有趣。

弗兰克：我只知道他是苏格兰人，23 岁时离开苏格兰去了美国。那是19 世纪 40 年代，铁路运输正兴旺起来。

格蕾丝：噢。我猜那时火车上也有很多盗窃案。

弗兰克：你说了我想说的话，所以他的侦探事务所破了很多这些案件，最后他终于见到了亚伯拉罕·林肯。

格蕾丝：之后他怎么样了呢？

弗兰克：这可怜的家伙滑倒了，不慎咬到了自己的舌头，后来死于细菌感染。

格蕾丝：真悲哀，他这么聪明。

弗兰克：是啊，真可惜！

跨文化交际小常识

在美国，急救的有效措施有：一、公民反应（citizen response），即现场公民首先识别发生了什么，然后快速拨打911急救电话或通知附近的第一反应者（first responder, FR），如警察、保安等，从而启动急救医疗服务体系。公民反应人员在最初数分钟内提供的救护非常关键，往往是救命的黄金时刻。二、急救医疗服务系统的快速启动（rapid activation of EMS），即指挥调度中心的调度人员接到现场求救电话后，迅速判断求救者需要何种救助，然后立即派遣适当的专业急救人员。三、第一反应者提供的救护，即第一个抵达现场且接受过一定救护训练并获得培训相关证书的人员。四、高级院前救护（more advanced prehospital care），即医疗救护员抵达现场，为病人提供较高级别的救护及生命支持。五、院内救护（hospital care），即病人被送到医院急诊科后，急诊科工作人员迅速接管病人，着手进一步的诊断和治疗。

读书笔记

Section 2　Intermediate 中级进阶

万用表达一览

☐ **set in** 设在

☐ **all sorts of** 各种各样的，形形色色的

☐ **like the fact that** 就像……的事

☐ **figure things out** 把事情弄清楚

☐ **every nook and cranny** 每个角落，犄角旮旯

☐ **keep a blog on** 坚持在博客上写

☐ **Sure thing!** 没问题！当然可以！

☐ **have a look** 看一看，看一眼

万用表达详解

1. **set in**

   释 take place in 设在

   例 The movie is set in modern-day Spain with flashbacks to the 1950's.

   这部电影讲的是现代西班牙的故事，其中重现了一些 50 年代的场景。

2. **all sorts of**

   释 many kinds of /many types of 各种各样的，形形色色的

   例 There are all sorts of rumors circulating. It's hard to tell what's true and what's not.

   有各种谣言流传，很难分辨孰真孰假。

3. **like the fact that**

   释 the matter of 就像……的事

   例 I have one pet peeve, like the fact that you never called me to wish me a happy birthday.

有件事我忍不了，就是你从不给我打电话祝我生日快乐。

4. **figure things out**

释 solve a problem/grasp an issue/matter 把事情弄清楚

例 At some point, you'll figure things out for yourself.

将来的某个时候你自己会弄明白的。

5. **every nook and cranny**

释 every inch of a place 每个角落，犄角旮旯

例 He knows every nook and cranny of this place.

他知道这个地方的每个角落。

6. **keep a blog on**

释 maintain a blog on 坚持在博客上写

例 I used to keep a blog on my activities abroad.

我过去常常坚持在博客上写自己在国外的生活。

7. **Sure thing!**

释 Sure!/Of course!/You bet! 没问题！当然可以！

例 A: Make sure you switch off all the electrical equipment before you leave.

离开前你一定要关掉所有的电器电源。

B: Sure thing!

没问题！

8. **have a look**

释 look at/have a gander at 看一看，看一眼

例 A: Let me have a look at that photo! I've seen this before somewhere.

让我看看那张照片！我以前在哪儿见过。

B: Yeah. It's the Space Needle in Seattle, Washington.

是啊，那是华盛顿省西雅图市的太空针塔。

实用对话场景

Grace: I was watching a TV show based on the Sherlock Holmes stories. But it's **set in** modern London. It's really funny.

Frank: Yeah. I know the one you mean. What was it called again? Oh yeah. *Sherlock*. I watched all the repeats.

Grace: Sherlock and Dr. Watson live together in a bachelor pad and have **all sorts of** adventures. They're really funny together. Superb acting too!

Frank: I really admire **the fact that** he's so knowledgeable and so savvy. He **figures things Out** at lightning speed...

Grace: Almost as if his brain were a computer. He knows **every nook and cranny** in London, but he doesn't know that the earth orbits the sun. That's funny!

Frank: Yeah. And what I think is hilarious is that Dr. Watson **keeps a blog on** their lives, and everyone at the police precinct reads it.

Grace: Did you see the episode where he met Moriarty? That was good.

Frank: Hey, let me know if you have any more episodes on your flash drive.

Grace: **Sure thing**! I'll **have a look** later on and send them to you.

格蕾丝：我刚才在看一部取材于福尔摩斯故事的电视剧，不过它是以现代伦敦为背景。这部剧真的很有趣。

弗兰克：嗯，我知道你指的这部。那叫什么来着？啊！对，叫《夏洛克》。所有的重播我都看了。

格蕾丝：夏洛克和华生医生一起住在一间单身公寓里，经历各种各样的奇遇。他们在一起真的很有趣，演技也非常出色！

弗兰克：他知识那么渊博、聪敏睿智，这一点我真的很羡慕。他以闪电般的速度把事情弄清楚……

格蕾丝：好像他的脑袋是个电脑一样，他知道伦敦的每一个犄角旮旯，但不知道地球绕着太阳转。好搞笑。

弗兰克：是啊，华生医生还坚持在博客上写他们的生活，警察分局的每个人都读，我觉得很滑稽。

格蕾丝：你看了他见到莫里亚蒂的那集没有？那集好看。

弗兰克：嘿，如果你的 U 盘里有其他集，记得告诉我啊！

格蕾丝：没问题！等会儿我看看吧，然后发给你。

跨文化交际小常识

　　现代啦啦队运动的历史可以追溯到19世纪80年代，当时美国正风行橄榄球，在普林斯顿大学的一场橄榄球赛场上，为了给队员加油，第一次出现了自发的有组织的团队表演形式，即现代啦啦队的雏形。现代啦啦队融入了越来越多的新鲜元素，比如舞蹈（dance）、口号（cheer）、舞伴特技（partner stunts）、叠罗汉（pyramid）、跳跃（jump）等动作技术，配合音乐、服装、队形变化及表示物品（如彩球、口号板、喇叭与旗帜）等，大幅提高了啦啦队表演的观赏力和号召力。

读书笔记

Section 3 ◆ Advanced 高级飞跃

万用表达一览

- [ ] **well-up on** 能够与时俱进，对……很在行
- [ ] **square with/jibe with** 符合，同……一致
- [ ] **uncanny knack for/of** 诀窍，特殊能力
- [ ] **a cinch for** 易如反掌的事，容易的事
- [ ] **come across as/like** 给人……印象，表现的像……
- [ ] **slip up** 疏忽
- [ ] **show his true colors** 现出原形；露出本来面目
- [ ] **throw him off the scent** 使某人失去线索，给某人提供错误信息
- [ ] **part of his act** 行为的一部分，装出来的
- [ ] **His instincts always prove to be correct.** 他的直觉（被证明）是正确的。
- [ ] **Likewise.** 同样地，（表示感觉相同的）我也是。

万用表达详解

1. well-up on

> 释 well informed about 能够与时俱进，对……很在行

> 例 A: Are you ready to talk about the new product?
>
> 你准备好讨论新产品了吗？
>
> B: I'm not too well-up on it. Give me some time to read over the promotional material first.
>
> 这个我不是很了解，给我点时间来熟读这些宣传资料吧。

2. square with/jibe with

> 释 correlate with/correspond with/match 符合，同……一致

> 例 His story just doesn't square with the facts.
>
> 他的故事与事实不符。

3. **uncanny knack for/of**

释 unusual ability to do sth. 诀窍，特殊能力

例 He has an uncanny knack for figuring out the most complicated problems.

在解决特别棘手的问题时，他总是有自己的诀窍。

4. **a cinch for**

释 easy for 易如反掌的事，容易的事

例 It should be a cinch for him to win. After all he's been training for this event for the last 4 years.

获胜对他来说易如反掌，毕竟在过去4年，他一直接受这种训练。

5. **come across as/like**

释 behave like. 给人……印象，表现的像……

例 He comes across as a rather self-important, arrogant individual.

他表现得相当妄自尊大，自命不凡。

6. **slip up**

释 make a mistake 疏忽

例 The thieves slipped up after unwittingly leaving their fingerprints all over the ATM machine, when they had attempted to rob.

窃贼一时疏忽，在试图抢劫时，无意中在ATM机上留下了指纹。

7. **show his true colors**

释 show his true personalities 现出原形；露出本来面目

例 The suspect showed his true colors when he attempted to cover up his crime.

嫌疑犯在掩饰自己的罪行时，反倒露出了本来的面目。

8. **throw him off the scent**

释 throw him off the trail 使某人失去线索，给某人提供错误信息

例 The escaped convict couldn't throw the dogs off the scent.

这个逃犯逃不过警犬的鼻子。

9. **part of his act**

释 part of his assumed character 行为的一部分，装出来的

例 Just keep in mind when you meet him he'll do things to unnerve you. It's all part of his act. He's just a little eccentric.

记住，当你见到他时，他会做一些事来吓唬你。他总是这样，就是有点怪。

10. **His instincts always prove to be correct.**

释 His intuition never failed him/His intuition was always correct.

他的直觉（被证明）是正确的。

例 My instincts in this case proved to be correct.

事实证明，我对这个案件的直觉是对的。

11. **Likewise.**

释 Same to you/Same here 同样地，（表示感觉相同的）我也是。

例 A: Happy hunting!

一帆风顺！

B: Likewise.

你也是！

实用对话场景

Grace: What comes to mind when you think of the word "detective"?

Frank: Well, several things come to mind. Sherlock Holmes for one. You know him, right? He's what you call a real "detective's detective". He's what many detectives aspire to be: debonair, clever, intellectual, definitely elitist, **well-up on** current affairs, elegant, a good conversationalist, and always successful in catching the criminal, no matter how clever he is.

Grace: Wow. That's a pretty good description of Sherlock Holmes.

Frank: You know, Hollywood has always portrayed Sherlock Holmes as a sporting type, a kind of macho detective, along with all the other attributes I just mentioned. I'm not so sure if the Hollywood portrayal **squares with** the original Sherlock character. But I do understand why he's so popular with so many readers, after a century or more, since Arthur Conan Doyle created him.

Grace: You're right about his popularity and I'll tell you why. We're fascinated by his attention to details, and his **uncanny knack for** discovering the most elusive and minute evidence to back up his theories. Crimes that baffle his peers are **a cinch for** Holmes to solve. That's why he's so revered among story detective characters to this day.

Frank: That brings me to the famous American TV detective character Colombo. He's like Sherlock's country cousin. His manners are clumsy and somewhat uncouth. He's respectful but comes across as a dim-wit. Nevertheless he always catches the suspect, largely because of the suspect's mistaken impression that the detective is harmless.

Grace: Ah, I see. It's because Colombo **comes across as** harmless that the suspect **slips up** and **shows his true colors** early.

Frank: That's right. The suspect underestimates Columbo's powers of perception. All the while, he's investigating and pursuing leads. If he comes close to discovering something, the suspect tries to **throw him off the scent**, by creating false leads to elude capture. Some of the TV episodes seem a little far-fetched, and he does seem a little too trusting for an experienced detective, but that's all **part of his act**. **His instincts always prove to be correct**.

Grace: He's by no means an idiot as what you're saying.

Frank: Right. The suspect is just no match for the sharp-witted Columbo.

Grace: Have you ever noticed in these old TV detective shows that these cases never come to trial? But in today's TV programs, once the detective has solved his case, there is often a quick trial and conviction of the suspect.

Frank: That's because of the times we live in. The TV audience today wants to see a conviction after an arrest.

Grace: I've also noticed that criminal investigation programs made for TV focus more on the science end of investigations.

Frank: Yes, that's because of this fascination many people have with science. Science is cool. Finding minute traces of blood, hair or skin, by using the most advanced techniques, guarantees a huge audience and popular ratings.

Grace: We often forget when we're watching these programs that a lot of these so called "advanced scientific techniques" are still science fiction.

Frank: That's a good point. Defense attorneys, defendants, judges, plaintiffs and prosecutors put on a good show in the TV courtroom, but in reality it's much more mundane and not particularly exciting to watch an analysis of a crime.

Grace: This has really been a fascinating conversation. I look forward to our next one.

Frank: **_Likewise._**

格蕾丝：当你想起"侦探"这个词的时候，会想到什么？

弗兰克：嗯，想到一些，夏洛克·福尔摩斯就是其中一个。你知道他是谁吧？他就是所谓真正的"侦探中的侦探"。他是许多侦探的偶像，他温文尔雅、聪明、睿智、超凡优秀、识时事、优雅、健谈，并且，不管罪犯多么狡猾，他总能将其成功抓获。

格蕾丝：哇，这是对福尔摩斯一个完美的描述。

弗兰克：你知道，除了我刚才提到的所有特质之外，好莱坞还把夏洛克·福尔摩斯描绘成一个运动型、有男子气概的侦探。我不是那么肯定好莱坞的描绘与原故事是否一致，但我的确明白为什么在阿瑟·柯南·道尔塑造了这个人物一个世纪以后，他仍然受到那么多读者的青睐。

格蕾丝：关于他的知名度你说得对，我来告诉你为什么。福尔摩斯非常注重细节，他还有一个不可思议的本领，就是能从蛛丝马迹中发现犯罪证据来支持他的推理，这让我们很着迷。侦破那些令他的同行们困惑的案件对福尔摩斯来说易如反掌。这就是为什么直到今天他在众多侦探故事人物中一直备受推崇的原因。

弗兰克：这让我想起了美国电视里著名的侦探人物哥伦布。他就像是另一个福尔摩斯，但却是另一副形象，像个乡巴佬。他举止笨拙，甚至有些粗野。他很谦恭，但却给人一个傻瓜的印象。尽管如此，他始终能顺利抓住疑犯，这主要是因为疑犯对于这样的一位侦探总会有错觉——这样的侦探对他们是没有威胁的。

格蕾丝：啊，我明白了。正是因为哥伦布给人一种"无威胁"的印象，才使犯罪嫌疑人掉以轻心，很快地暴露真面目。

弗兰克：是的，疑犯低估了哥伦布的感知力。一直以来他都在调查和寻找线索。如果他快要找到新的线索，犯罪嫌疑人就会制造假象来迷惑他，从而避免被逮捕。有些电视情节似乎有点令人难以置信，而且作为一个有经验的侦探，他也似乎有点过于轻信那些线索，但这一切就是他行为全部，事实证明他的直觉总是对的。

格蕾丝：他绝不是你说的什么傻子。

弗兰克：对。疑犯不可能是这么聪敏的哥伦布的对手。

格蕾丝：你注意到没有，在老侦探系列剧中，这些案件从未审判过，但在今天的电视剧中，一旦案件被侦破，疑犯往往会很快被审判并定罪。

弗兰克：这是由我们所处的时代决定的。今天的电视观众希望看到逮捕疑犯后将其定罪。

格蕾丝：我也注意到，如今电视剧里的刑事调查，更关注调查的科技性。

弗兰克：是的，这是因为有很多人迷恋科技的魔力。科技太酷了！用最先进的技术查出极微小的血迹、头发或皮肤，就可以保证有很高的观众收视率。

格蕾丝：不过我们在看这些所谓"先进科技"节目时，会常常忘记这些技术还只存在于科幻小说中。

弗兰克：还真是。辩护律师、被告、法官、原告和检察官在电视法庭上共同上演一出好戏。但在现实中，所有一切都是那么平常，观看犯罪分析也并不那么让人兴奋。

格蕾丝：这次谈话很有意思，我期待下次有机会再聊。

弗兰克：我也是。

跨文化交际小常识

　　高尔夫球运动比赛球员2～4人一组，在球场的发球区依次用高尔夫球杆把各自的球击出后，一起经球道等走向球的落点，继续击球，直至将球击入洞内。击球的标准杆数一般为72杆，以击球杆数少者为胜。比赛如为四轮72个球洞时，在18个球洞的球场上需循环四次。高尔夫球的计分方法有两种：一为比赛所有洞穴的总击球数，少者为胜；二为比赛每个洞穴的击球数，包括相等数，以击球次数少、洞穴多者为胜。目前，在亚洲、欧洲、美国和南非都有成功的职业高尔夫球巡回赛，其中英国公开赛（The Open Championship）、大师锦标赛（Masters Tournament，也称名人赛，即The Masters）、美国公开赛（United States Open Championship）和PGA锦标赛（PGA Championship，PGA=Professional Golfers' Association）是争夺最为激烈的四大赛事。

Unit 8 | Theater 戏剧

Section 1 Basic 初级基础

万用表达一览

- [ ] **lucky** 幸好
- [ ] **make it just in time** 正是时候
- [ ] **It's not surprising!** 不奇怪啊！不足为奇！
- [ ] **the lineup** 演员阵容；嫌疑人行列

万用表达详解

1. **lucky**

   释 good thing/fortunately 幸好

   例 Lucky we saved enough for the trip. It's going to set us back a few grand.

   幸好我们为这趟旅行存够钱了，要花掉我们好几千块呢。

2. **make it just in time**

   释 arrive just in time for 正是时候

   例 We made it just in time for the opening ceremony.

   我们正好赶上开幕式。

3. **It's not surprising!**

   释 It should come as no surprise/It shouldn't come as any surprise/It's no wonder 不奇怪啊！不足为奇！

   例 It's not surprising kids know so much these days. Parents want to prepare their kids for a tough and uncertain future.

现在的孩子知道很多东西，这一点都不奇怪。父母都想让自己的孩子做好准备去迎接一个艰难而不确定的未来。

4. **the lineup**

釋 ① the cast of actors; ② possible perpetrators at a police station lined up for identification 演员阵容；嫌疑人行列

例 The lineup at the event included all the famous stars from the movie and music industries.

出席这次盛典的包括了影视音乐界的所有著名明星。

实用对话场景

Helen: Wow! Look at this crowd. **Lucky** we booked our seats early.

Bill: Where are we sitting?

Helen: Third row, near the middle. We have a great view. It looks like we **made it just in time.**

Bill: Look, the curtain's opening. Listen to that applause!

Helen: **It's not surprising!** Look at **the lineup**. Hey, there's Kevin Spacey! I saw him in *Casino Jack*. Brilliant actor!

Bill: Now I'm excited. OK, let's watch!

(The show has ended...)

Helen: Well, that was something! Wait! They're coming out one more time together, for a final curtain call.

Bill: Well, I have to see this show again.

Helen: That makes two of us! It was worth every penny!

海伦：哇！看看这人群！幸好我们提前订了位。

比尔：我们的座位在哪儿？

海伦：第三排，靠中间，我们的座位很好啊，看来我们来得正是时候。

比尔：看，大幕拉开了。听，掌声！

海伦：不奇怪啊！看看这部话剧的主演阵容。嘿，有凯文·史派西，我在《政客杰克》里看过他，他是个很出色的演员！

比尔：现在我很兴奋。好了，我们看话剧吧。

（演出结束了）

海伦：哇！是部不错的话剧啊！等等，他们再次一起出来，最后谢幕了！

比尔：嗯，我一定要再看一遍这部戏。

海伦：我和你一样！这钱花得很值啊！

跨文化交际小常识干

　　曲棍球的出现要比最初的奥林匹克运动会早1200年或者更多。由于曲棍球在中国开展得比较晚，很多人对它还不是很了解。尽管如此，我国的曲棍球队在世界上还是蛮有竞争力的。国家女子曲棍球队就曾获得过第14届亚运会冠军、2004年雅典奥运会第四名以及2008年北京奥运会亚军的好成绩。曲棍球场地长91.40米，宽55米，球门高2.14米，宽3.66米，球棍长80~95厘米，球重156~163克。比赛时两队各11名运动员上场。全场比赛时间为70分钟，分上、下两个半时，中间休息5~10分钟。进一球得一分，以射入对方球门多者为胜。在球场上，运动员左手握棍把，右手握球棍的中上部。上场队员不得穿带有铁钉的鞋或佩戴对其他队员可能造成危险的物品，必须戴护腿板。守门员应佩戴头盔、护脚、护腿、护身、护手以及保护上臂和肘部的护具。

读书笔记

Section 2　Intermediate 中级进阶

万用表达一览

☐ **What's the scoop?** 有什么特别新闻？有什么新鲜事？

☐ **hand in** 上交，提交

☐ **my entire view of** 对……的看法

万用表达详解

1. What's the scoop?

释 What recent/exclusive news do you have? 有什么特别新闻？
有什么新鲜事？

例 A: What's the scoop?

有什么新鲜事儿？

B: I just got my results! I'm on cloud nine!

我刚刚知道成绩！好开心啊！

2. hand in

释 to submit a paper/homework/assignment etc. to a teacher
上交，提交

例 A: I need to hand in this paper tomorrow morning, but I can't
think of anything to write.

我明早就要交这篇论文了，但我还没想到要写什么。

B: Writer's block, eh?

文思堵塞？

3. my entire view of

释 my whole view/opinion 对……的看法

例 My entire view of education was formed here. It's the only
one I've ever known.

我的整个教育观都是在这里形成的，这是我关于教育的唯一观点。

 实用对话场景

Helen: So **what's the scoop** from school today?

Bill: We have to **hand in** a paper about theater tomorrow, but I'm really drawing a blank right now!

Helen: Ancient or modern theater?

Bill: Modern theater.

Helen: Hmmm. Well, I just saw a one-man show called "*Twain*". It was a very good performance, especially the sound and lighting... Very cinematic.

Bill: Let me guess! The play was about the writer Mark Twain.

Helen: Yes, and it changed **my entire view of** theater. I never thought theater could be mass entertainment. Watching "*Twain*" was like watching a movie. You know, he traveled all over the world, and the special effects for the Mississippi River, Palestine and Hawaii were very realistic.

Bill: Hey, I think I have the starting paragraph in my head now.

Helen: Let me know if you need any help.

Bill: Will do!

海伦：今天学校里有什么特别新闻？

比尔：我们明天要交一篇关于戏剧的论文，但现在我的脑子里真的是一片空白！

海伦：古代还是现代剧？

比尔：现代剧。

海伦：呃，我刚看过一部叫《吐温》的独角戏。那个表演很好，特别是声效和光效……很有电影的感觉。

比尔：让我想想。这部戏剧是关于作家马克·吐温的。

海伦：是的，它完全改变了我对戏剧的看法。我从来没想过戏剧可以是一种大众娱乐方式，看《吐温》就像看电影一样。你知道他

到处游历，而且剧中密西西比河、巴勒斯坦和夏威夷的特效做得特别逼真。

比尔：嘿，现在我想我已经知道怎么开始了。

海伦：如果你需要帮忙的话，跟我说。

比尔：会的！

跨文化交际小常识

在西方，男女理发店是分开的。一般来说，美国的男士女士理发店（barber shop）费用都很高，而且大都需要打电话预约。洗头、烫发、剪发和整发都是单项分开收费，最后还要加上10%~15%的小费（tips）。所以，很多美国人都选择在家里让家人给自己剪发，既方便快捷，也省钱。此外，在包括美国在内的西方许多国家，只有考取了理发师执照（the barber's license）或美容师执照（cosmetologist's license）的人才有资格开理发店，否则便是违法的。

读书笔记

Section 3 Advanced 高级飞跃

万用表达一览

☐ **more of a draw** 更具吸引力

☐ **This is why/That's why/Which is why/That explains why...** 这就
是为什么 / 这就解释了为什么

☐ **feels much more like** 感觉更像……

☐ **give the illusion** 让你产生幻觉，给你错觉

☐ **staple feature** 主要特色，共同特点

☐ **all walks of life** 各个阶层，各种背景，各行各业

☐ **perfect place for** 最佳地点，最好的地方

☐ **sleight of hand** 巧妙手法

☐ **serve a necessary function** 发挥着必要的作用

☐ **it's best to** 最好是

☐ **Failing that...** 如果没有

万用表达详解

1. **more of a draw**

   释 more of an attraction 更具吸引力

   例 I think Shanghai is probably more of a draw for tourists than
   Guangzhou.

   我想对游客来说，上海比广州更具有吸引力。

2. **This is why/That's why/Which is why/That explains why...**

   释 This is the reason for... 这就是为什么 / 这就解释了为什么

   例 A: Every day he comes home exhausted and then stays up all
   night.

   每天他回来的时候就已经精疲力竭了，然后还通宵不睡。

B: That's why he is always late for work.

这就是他为什么总是上班迟到的原因。

3. **feels much more like**

释 The feeling I get is a lot more like 感觉更像……

例 This weather feels much more like spring than summer.

这种天气感觉更像是春天而不是夏天。

4. **give the illusion**

释 give the false impression that 让你产生幻觉，给你错觉

例 A: These clothes will give everyone the illusion that you're slim.

这些衣服很显瘦。

B: That's the whole idea!

这就是我想要的效果！

5. **staple feature**

释 everyday normal part of 主要特色，共同特点

例 Reading to others used to be a staple feature of home entertainment before TV and radio.

在电视和收音机问世之前，读书给其他人听是家庭娱乐的一个主要特色。

6. **all walks of life**

释 all kinds of backgrounds 各个阶层，各种背景，各行各业

例 You will meet people there from all walks of life.

在那儿你可以见到各行各业的人。

7. **perfect place for**

释 ideal venue/ideal location for 最佳地点，最好的地方

例 This would be a perfect place for a shop.

这也许是开商店的最佳地点。

8. **sleight of hand**

释 any artful trick/skill in deception 巧妙手法

例 The magician pulled off the trick with an uncanny sleight of hand.
魔术师用不可思议的巧妙手法变出了这个魔术。

9. serve a necessary function

释 have a necessary role to play 发挥着必要的作用

例 The traffic police serve a necessary function. They make sure drivers follow the rules of the road.
交通警察发挥着重要的作用，他们确保司机遵守交通规则。

10. it's best to

释 the best thing to do is 最好是

例 It's best to sometimes let things go, rather than stay angry at them forever.
有时最好顺其自然，不要老跟他们生气。

11. Failing that...

释 If that doesn't work 如果没有

例 A: Try pulling your arm out slowly.
试着把你的胳膊慢慢拽出来。

B: I can't. It's stuck.
拽不出来，粘住了。

A: Try putting some of this grease on it to ease it out. Failing that, I'll call the fire brigade.
试着把这些润滑油倒进去，看有没有用。如果还不行，我就叫消防队了。

实用对话场景

Helen: If you ask me, I'd say that the theater is becoming *more of a draw* for people who enjoy spectacle as well as more refined entertainment.

Bill: Why is that?

Helen: Well, because so many people have grown up with so much mass entertainment, offering instant gratification, theaters need to do the same if they want to stay in business.

Bill: So you're saying that people don't want to sit for two or three hours pondering the virtues or vices of a character on a stage. They want lights, action and uproariously funny situations, just like they get in the movies.

Helen: Yes. **This is why** going to the theater these days **feels much more like** a "live" movie. The kinds of shows people go to see these days, have many of the effects you see in movies.

Bill: You're right. There are stunts, special effects, and computer-generated images to dazzle you, put you in suspense or **give** you **the illusion** of reality.

Helen: Right. Magic shows, for example, are a **staple feature** of theater these days. Magic attracts people from **all walks of life** and educational backgrounds. A theater is a **perfect place for** this kind of entertainment.

Bill: You're right. It's both spectacle and art. The magician's **sleight of hand** is the real attraction.

Helen: So theaters **serve a necessary function** in towns and cities around the country.

Bill: In what way?

Helen: Well, they serve as both cultural institutions and places of entertainment, without the crude elements found in many movies on the market today.

Bill: You have a point. By the way, where's the best place to sit in a theater, would you say?

Helen: Without a doubt, **it's best to** sit somewhere near the stage, but not too close, so you get a good enough view of the actors and their expressions on stage. **Failing that**, you should try to

get center seats. Enjoy the show!
 Bill: I will. And thanks for the tip.
Helen: Anytime.

海伦：如果你问我，我想说戏剧对热爱壮观场面以及高雅艺术的人们越来越具吸引力了。

比尔：这是为什么？

海伦：嗯，因为现在很多人在成长的过程中被大众娱乐所包围，这些能给人一种即时的满足感，所以剧院要想立足，就得这么做。

比尔：所以你是说观众不想坐两三个小时深思舞台上角色的美德或恶习。他们需要灯光、动作以及滑稽可笑的场景，就像他们身处电影中一样。

海伦：是的，这就是为什么如今去剧院的感觉更像看一场"活生生"的电影。现在人们看到的这种表演中有很多你能在电影里看到的特效。

比尔：你说得对。特技、特效、电脑合成图像，能够让你眼花缭乱，将你引入悬念，让你产生幻觉。

海伦：是的。比如说，如今，魔术表演是剧院的主要特色，魔术吸引了来自各阶层的人们，剧院是此类娱乐的理想场所。

比尔：你说得对，这是壮观的场景和艺术魅力的结合。魔术师的戏法很有吸引力。

海伦：因此，剧院在全国各城镇发挥着必要的作用。

比尔：以什么方式？

海伦：它们既是文化服务机构又是娱乐场所，而且它们没有目前市场上许多电影中都有的那些粗俗的元素。

比尔：你说得很对。顺便问一下，剧院最好的座位是在哪里？你能告诉我吗？

海伦：毫无疑问，最好坐在靠近舞台的位置，这样你就能清楚地看到舞台上的演员和他们的面部表情了，但也不要离得太近。如果没有，那也应该设法坐在中间的座位上。好好欣赏节目吧！

比尔：我会的，感谢你的建议。

海伦：不用客气。

跨文化交际小常识

　　路边停车位是纽约市政府设立和管理的，收费相对较低，规定也非常严格。对停车地点、时段、时限和收费标准，都做了严格的规定。一般在纽约市商业区及主要街道，随处可见停车计时器，供开车人短时间停车使用，通常最多可停两小时。如超过规定时间还没有将车开走，巡视的管理人员就会将罚单贴在车窗上。路边停车的收费标准也根据地段不同而各有差异：市中心繁华地带一般为每小时1～2美元或更高，而在不太繁华的地方1小时收费为25美分。为了满足人们的需求，纽约市区内还兴建了不少停车场。这种停车场大多是公司经营的，定价完全根据市场需求来决定，收费相对较高，每小时收费从十几美元到20多美元不等，一些黄金地段停车场的收费在全美国都是最高的。

读书笔记

Unit 9 | Hair Care 头发护理

万用表达一览

☐ **nice and short** 简洁
☐ **in the back** 在后面
☐ **nice and even** 平整，不歪斜

万用表达详解

1. nice and short

释 short and sweet 简洁

例 He kept his e-mails nice and short.
他把电子邮件写得很简洁。

2. in the back

释 at the back/in the rear 在后面

例 The students lounging around in the back of the class fared much worse than those sitting up front.
坐在教室后面的学生比坐在前面的表现要差很多。

3. nice and even

释 even/not crooked 均匀，平整，不歪斜

例 Make sure the spacing between your words on the page is nice and even.
确保页面上的字距均匀美观一些。

Jane: Hi. What can I do for you?

Alan: Just a dry cut please. **Nice and short.** Make sure you cut above the ears and square the back. I don't want a rounded cut **in the back**. Don't take too much off the top.

Jane: Are you sure you don't want a wash first?

Alan: No thanks. Use the shears. It's faster.

Jane: You sound like you're in a hurry.

Alan: Yeah. I have to be somewhere in about 20 minutes, and I don't want to look shaggy.

Jane: Do you want a shave as well?

Alan: Just the back of the neck please. **Nice and even** please.

Jane: OK. All done.

Alan: What do I owe you?

Jane: That'll be 20 bucks.

Alan: 20, it is. Thanks.

简：你好，有什么我可以帮你吗？

艾伦：麻烦你不要洗，直接剪短就好。剪得好一点，短一点，一定要剪到耳朵上面，后面要剪整齐，我可不想后面剪得圆圆的，上面别剪太多。

简：你确定你不先洗头发？

艾伦：不用了，谢谢。用电动剃头机吧，那样快一点。

简：听起来你很赶时间。

艾伦：是的，大约 20 分钟后我要去一个地方，我不想头发看起来乱糟糟的。

简：需要剃胡须吗？

艾伦：只剃脖子后面的。请剃得平整、好看一些。

简：好的，搞定了。

艾伦：我要付你多少钱？

简：20 美元。

艾伦：这是 20 美元，谢谢。

跨文化交际小常识

　　提起发达的美国电影，人们脑海里会浮现许多不同的类型，比如爱情片、喜剧片、音乐歌舞片、侦探片、强盗片、灾难片等。其中，以反映美国人精神倾向为代表的西部片（western movies），在历经了繁荣与衰退的起伏之后，成了一个延续近百年的神话，备受文艺青年和老人的喜爱。在经典的西部片中，人们总是被那些孤身抗暴的牛仔、试图建立和维护法律的警察、贞洁的女主角、善良的男主角、甚至邪恶的歹徒所深深吸引。无论是影片里荒凉的喀斯特地貌、陡峭的山谷和印第安人的营地，还是简陋的驿站、酒馆和原木小屋，置身其中的来复枪、马匹、马靴、宽边帽、牛仔服和皮裤等都能让观众无比震撼。

读书笔记

Section 2　Intermediate 中级进阶

万用表达一览

☐ **Why not...** 为什么不……

☐ **It suits you.** 很适合你。

☐ **down the road** ①在那里，在路的那一头；② 将来某个时候

☐ **Trust me on this.** 在这点上相信我吧。

☐ **I know first hand.** 从我切身经验中知道。

☐ **check out** 看看，核实

☐ **a real hack job** 真糟糕

☐ **Don't say I didn't warn you!** 别说我没提醒过你!

万用表达详解

1. **Why not...**

   释 Why don't you... 为什么不……

   例 Why not see the show for yourself? That way you can tell us all first hand how it went.

   为什么你不亲自去看表演? 那样你就可以直接告诉我们剧情了。

2. **It suits you.**

   释 It's right for you. 很适合你。

   例 A: I don't like the outfit.

   　　我不喜欢这套行头。

   　　B: Why not? It suits you!

   　　为什么不呢? 很适合你!

3. **down the road**

   释 ① further along the road 在那里，在路的那一头；② later in the future 将来某个时候

例 There is a throng of people waiting in line down the road.

马路的那一边有一群人在排队。

4. **Trust me on this.**

释 Believe me, when I tell you this. 在这点上相信我吧。

例 You're doing the right thing! Trust me on this!

你在做正确的事！这点相信我吧！

5. **I know first hand.**

释 I know from experience. 从我切身经验中知道。

例 I know first hand what you're talking about.

我有切身经验，所以能明白你说的话。

6. **check out**

释 look at 看看，核实

例 Check out the latest statistics on "summa cum laude" graduates from these universities.

看看这些大学最优成绩毕业生的最新统计数据。

7. **a real hack job**

释 a real mess 真糟糕

例 That book is a real hack job. Just look at the quality of the writing.

那本书真糟糕，看看写作的质量就知道了。

8. **Don't say I didn't warn you!**

释 expressed after warning someone 别说我没提醒过你！

例 He's in an awful mood today. Don't say I didn't warn you!

今天他的心情很不好，别说我没提醒过你！

实用对话场景

Jane: I need a haircut.

Alan: **Why not** let it grow? **It suits you.**

Jane: No. Not in this weather. It's too hot for long hair. I feel cooler if my hair is short.

Alan: Don't go to that place **down the road**, though. They think every customer wants hair styles like theirs. **Trust me on this**. **I know first hand**. Here! **Check out** this photo. That was 4 months ago.

Jane: Oh, my God. Why is your hair red? They did **a real hack job** on you. I don't notice it now, though.

Alan: Never again! **Don't say I didn't warn you** about them.

Jane: OK. Noted! What about that hair salon around the corner?

Alan: BBs? Yeah. They're all right. Just tip them nicely, and they'll be extra nice to you.

Jane: OK. I've got to run. See you.

简：我要剪发。

艾伦：为什么不留长呢？那很适合你。

简：不，这种天气不要了吧，太热了，不适合留长头发。我觉得短头发更凉爽些。

艾伦：不要去这条路上的那间理发店，他们认为每个顾客都想要和他们一样的发型，这点你相信我吧，我有切身经历的。来！看看我这张照片，那是 4 个月以前的。

简：噢，天啊，你的头发为什么是红色的？他们把你弄得真难看。但现在我看不出来啊。

艾伦：再也不去了！别说我没有提醒过你。

简：好的，记住了！那角落的理发店怎样？

艾伦：BBs？嗯，他们可以，多给他们一点小费，他们会弄得特别好的。

简：好的，我要走了，再见。

跨文化交际小常识

问路是到达目的地最省事、最有效的办法。在英美国家，人们对于外国人问路通常会热心回答的。但在问话时，他们不喜欢你一口气很流利地背出许多问话，也不喜欢在别人思考你的问题时一直追问，更不喜欢陌生人离他们太近，这样会使他们觉得很不自在，甚至觉得是一种威胁，因为西方人的空间意识很强。向人问路时，一般都会说句Excuse me，一方面可以引起对方注意，另一方面也比较客气有礼貌一些。如果没有听清，可以说 I beg your pardon?（用升调，意为：对不起，我没听清）或者说I'm afraid I didn't quite catch you.（请再说一遍好吗？我恐怕没有完全听清）。问完路后，应向指路人表示感谢。

读书笔记

Section 3 • Advanced 高级飞跃

万用表达一览

☐ **There's no getting around it.** 你必须面对，你不能避开它。

☐ **overall appearance** 整体外观

☐ **other than** 除了

☐ **by far one of the most** 迄今为止最……之一，（相对于其他）最……

☐ **take great care** 非常小心地呵护

☐ **keep it in good shape** 尽量保持良好的状态

☐ **eventually** 最终

☐ **not just yet** 不是现在

☐ **Touch wood...** 但愿走好运，但愿吉利

☐ **You're all set!** 大功告成！

☐ **Don't even dream of it!** 你想都不要想！／你别做梦了！

万用表达详解

1. **There's no getting around it.**

   释 You can't avoid it. /There's no escaping it. 你必须面对，你不能避开它。

   例 There's no getting around it. We're all getting older.
   我们都在变老，这是不能避免的。

2. **overall appearance**

   释 someone's general appearance 整体外观

   例 His overall appearance is disheveled.
   他整个人看上去很邋遢。

3. **other than**

   释 apart from 除了

   例 A: Can you remember anything about her?

你能想起关于她的什么吗？

B: Other than her face, nothing else comes to mind.

除了她的脸，其他的什么都记不起来了。

4. by far one of the most

释 expresses "extremely" 迄今为止最……之一，（相对于其他）最……

例 He is by far the most trustworthy individual I've ever met.

他是我目前为止见过的最值得信任的人。

5. take great care

释 be extremely careful 非常小心地呵护

例 Take great care while handling that glass. It's very fragile.

拿那个杯子的时候要格外小心，易碎。

6. keep it in good shape

释 maintain health/fitness/stay in good shape 尽量保持良好的状态

例 I try to keep in good shape, but it's not that easy.

我尝试保持体形，但并不那么容易啊。

7. eventually

释 in the end/finally 最终

例 Eventually, you're all going to have to cut back on your spending.

最终，你们都得缩减开支。

8. not just yet

释 not right now/not at this moment in time 不是现在

例 A: Are you ready to retire?

你快要退休了吗？

B: Not just yet!

现在还没有！

9. Touch wood...

释 Fingers crossed! Wish me luck! Let's hope so! 但愿走好运，但愿吉利

例 Touch wood we win tomorrow!

但愿我们明天能获胜!

10. You're all set!

释 You are all ready. Also expressed by a shopkeeper/salesperson after completing a sale/service 大功告成!

例 A: OK. You're all set! Anything else?

好吧! 大功告成了! 还有其他事吗?

B: No. That's it. Thanks.

没有了,谢谢!

11. Don't even dream of it!

释 expressed toward people off doing sth. Don't get any ideas!

你想都不要想! / 你别做梦了!

例 A: Do you mind if I borrow your iPhone?

你介意我借用一下你的 iPhone 吗?

B: Don't even dream of it!

你别做梦了!

实用对话场景

Jane: I'd like a haircut please.

Alan: How would you like it?

Jane: Short but not too short. Short on the sides and back. Not too short on top.

Alan: How's that?

Jane: It's still a little long. Can you cut it a little shorter here...and there?

Alan: No problem. Won't be a minute! How about a wash?

Jane: No need to wash my hair. A little shorter in the back please.

Alan: That should do it. *You're all set.* You look terrific!

Jane: What did you do? That's a disaster! It's crooked! Straighten it please! What a mess! I can't leave looking like that.

Alan: Would you like a wig?

Jane: That's it. We're done. I'm leaving! And ***don't even dream*** of charging me!

简：我想理发。

艾伦：你想怎么剪？

简：剪短但不要太短，两边和后面剪短，上面不要太短。

艾伦：这样可以吗？

简：还是有点长，这里，还有那里，能给我再剪短些吗？

艾伦：没问题，马上就好！冲一下水好吗？

简：不用洗，后面请再剪短一点。

艾伦：这样就可以了，修好了！你看起来很棒！

简：你都做了什么？太可怕了！剪歪了，请弄齐了！真是糟透了！我不能这个样子出去。

艾伦：要不要戴假发？

简：就这样吧，再也不来了。走了！别想收我钱！

🎒 跨文化交际小常识

询问健康（Asking about health）：表示对某人健康情况的关心时，英美人不喜欢中国人带有劝告性的忠告，如"请多穿衣""多喝水"。他们认为这犹如家长的口气，并非出于关心。探望病人，英美人一般不送大礼，更不能送食品。他们喜欢送鲜花或慰问卡片或书、唱片等。在中国，对别人的健康状况表示关心是有教养、有礼貌的表现。但对西方人的健康表示关心，就不能按中国的传统方式了。一个中国学生得知其美籍教师生病后，会关切地说"you should go to see a doctor!（你应该到医院看看）。"不料，这句体贴的话反而使这位教师很不高兴。因为在这位教师看来，有病看医生这种简单的事情连小孩都知道，用不着任何人来指教。如果就某种小事给人以忠告，那显然是对其能力的怀疑，从而大大伤害其自尊心。

Unit 10

Health
健康

万用表达一览

☐ **This is all a dream.** 这只是个梦吧！

☐ **any minute/moment/second now** 一下子，再过几秒

☐ **This is it!** 就是这样！

☐ **put... foot down** 坚决反对

☐ **Way to go!** 真棒！好样的！

万用表达详解

1. **This is all a dream.**

   释 None of this is true/real. 这只是个梦吧！

   例 A: This is all a dream!

   　　这只是个梦吧！

   　　B: It's no dream. You won. Congratulations!

   　　不是梦，你赢了，恭喜你！

2. **any minute/moment/second now**

   释 any moment now 一下子，再过几秒

   例 Any second now, he'll come through that door. He's so consistent, and you can set your watch by him.

   再过几秒他就会进来了。他一直很守时，你可以当他是闹钟。

3. **This is it!**

   释 It expresses that "This is what we've been waiting for". 就是这样！

例 This is it! There's no going back now. We're in it for the long haul.

就这样！现在不能回到从前了，我们要长期坚持下去。

4. put... foot down

释 insist on an end to something intolerable 坚决反对

例 She put her foot down when they came back with more inane requests.

他们回来提出更愚蠢的要求时，她坚决反对。

5. Way to go!

释 Good job!/Fantastic!/Wonderful!/Excellent! 真棒！好样的！

例 A: I just scored top marks on my test.

我考试拿了第一。

B: Way to go!

好样的！

实用对话场景

Susan: This canteen food is great today. What happened?

Nick: New school policy. Fresh fruit and vege every day. Oh yeah and look... sandwiches.

Susan: Wow. **This is all a dream,** and I'm going to wake up **any minute now.**

Nick: It's no dream. **This is it!** The parents finally **put** their **foot down**. Do you see where all the snack vending machines used to be? All gone!

Susan: I'm going to miss my soda! Just kidding!

Nick: No more soda. Freshly-squeezed orange juice every day.

Susan: No way! **Way to go**!

苏珊：今天饭堂的食物很好吃，怎么回事？

尼克：学校新政策，每天要有新鲜蔬果。噢对了，瞧……三明治。

苏珊：哇，这只是个梦吧，随时会醒的。

尼克：不是梦，就是这样！是家长们最终坚决反对的。你看以前的那
　　　些零食自动贩卖机到哪儿去了吗？不见了！

苏珊：我会想念我的汽水的！开个玩笑！

尼克：不再有汽水了，每天鲜榨橙汁。

苏珊：不会吧！做得好！

📖 跨文化交际小常识

　　英美人不喜欢别人打听自己的私事。诸如年龄、婚姻状况、个
人收入、财产、宗教信仰、竞选中投谁的票等都属于个人的隐私，别
人无权知道。谁在这方面提出问题，他肯定会遭人厌恶。值得一提
的是，在英美国家，老年人绝对不喜欢别人恭维他们的年龄，而在我
国，老年人喜欢别人赞美自己长寿。

读书笔记

Section 2 　Intermediate 中级进阶

 **万用表达一览**

- [ ] **don't get me started** 别跟我提……
- [ ] **I think you're onto something!** 你的思路是对的，我觉得你想到什么了。
- [ ] **not as... as we might think** 没有像我们想的那样……
- [ ] **go overboard** 做得太过，走极端，鲁莽行事
- [ ] **Let's just say...** 我们这样说吧
- [ ] **with a grain of salt** 持保留态度
- [ ] **We could argue about this all day.** 我们可以一直争论这个问题。
- [ ] **a no-win situation** 只输不赢的局面，左右为难的境地，两面不讨好的境地
- [ ] **We're just going to have to agree to disagree...** 我们各自保留意见吧

万用表达详解

1. **don't get me started**

   释 don't let me start complaining 别跟我提……

   例 A: Our neighbor's dog is barking like crazy over something.
   我们邻居家的狗像发疯似的在叫。

   B: Oh. Don't get me started on dogs or we'll be here all day!
   噢，别跟我提狗了，不然我们要在这儿说上一整天呢！

2. **I think you're onto something!**

   释 I think you are on your way to discovering something (important / unique) 你的思路是对的，我觉得你想到什么了。

   例 A: We tweaked this formula a little and look what we discovered. It's a new formula!

我们稍微调整了这个方程式，看看我们发现什么了：一个新方程！

B: I think you're onto something!

我觉得你的思路是对的！

3. **not as... as we might think**

释 not as you think 没有像我们想的那样……

例 He's not as clever as you might think. He didn't invent anything new.

他没有你想的那样聪明，并没有发明什么新东西。

4. **go overboard**

释 go to extremes 做得太过，走极端，鲁莽行事

例 A: I don't want to go overboard here, but we need to get to Beijing by this evening.

我不想过于紧张了，但我们今晚一定要抵达北京。

B: Are you suggesting we fly there?

你在建议我们坐飞机到那儿吗？

A: I'm afraid we have no other choice. I don't think we'll make it there on time by train.

恐怕没有其他选择了，我觉得坐火车的话我们不能按时抵达。

5. **Let's just say...**

释 used when phrasing something delicately 我们这样说吧

例 A: You're worth a fortune now!

你现在身价很高哦！

B: Let's just say I've done well for myself.

这样说吧，我做得还不错。

6. **with a grain of salt**

释 pay little or no attention to 持保留态度

例 I take everything he says with a grain of salt and so should you.

我对他所说的都持保留态度，你也应该这样。

7. **We could argue about this all day.**

释 We could dispute that all day/forever 我们可以一直争论这个问题。

例 We could argue about this all day, but it doesn't change the fact that you need to change your approach to studying.
我们可以一直争论这个问题，但这改变不了你需要改变学习方法的事实。

8. **a no-win situation**

释 You're bound to lose whatever you do. 只输不赢的局面，左右为难的境地，两面不讨好的境地

例 I'm in a no-win situation. Either way I lose.
我根本赢不了，无论怎样我都输了。

9. **We're just going to have to agree to disagree...**

释 expressed after a stalemate in a discussion /argument that no one can win 我们各自保留意见吧

例 A: Neither of us is going to win this argument! We're just going to have to agree to disagree.
我们俩怎么争论都不会有什么结果的！我们各自保留意见吧。

B: Fine by me!
正合我意！

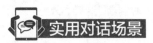 **实用对话场景**

Susan: We were discussing health in class today.

Nick: And? What were people saying?

Susan: The usual. "We're healthier and live longer than before". But I have my doubts that we're a lot healthier. It can't be true. After all, I see more young people smoking and eating more fast food than ever before. And ***don't get me started*** on obesity and diabetes in young people here!

Nick: *I think you're onto something!* A generation ago we did eat better than we do now. We're so used to eating canned and frozen food these days, and we even never consider that it's all processed and *not as natural as we might think.*

Susan: Exactly. If we don't see a skull-and-crossbones on the can of stew or frozen peas, it must be safe to eat, right? Wrong!

Nick: OK. Let's not *go overboard* here. *Let's just say* that canned and frozen food won't kill you, but there are healthier ways to eat. The thing is, many people just don't have the time anymore to prepare meals like your grandmother did.

Susan: OK. Granted! But what about farmers spraying their crops with pesticides or injecting their livestock with hormones and antibiotics? Is meat still safe to eat?

Nick: Well, that's why supermarkets stock organic products.

Susan: Don't get me started on organic! We have to take a lot of that industry *with a grain of salt.*

Nick: *We could argue about this all day.* It's really *a no-win situation*, unless you grow your own vegetables or raise your own livestock. But that's just not feasible for most of us.

Susan: *We're just going to have to agree to disagree* on this topic. One thing's for sure, though. The government needs to get involved.

苏珊：今天我们在课上讨论关于健康的话题。

尼克：那大家都说了些什么？

苏珊：跟往常一样，"我们比以前更健康、更长寿"，但我怀疑我们并不比以前健康很多。看看有更多年轻人抽烟，而且比以前吃更多快餐，就知道这不可能是真的，更别和我提年轻人患肥胖症和糖尿病了。

尼克：我觉得你说到点子上了！上个年代我们的确比现在吃得好。现在我们很习惯吃罐装和冷冻食物，我们甚至没想过，那些食物都是加工过的，可能没有我们想象的那样天然。

苏珊：正是。如果我们在炖肉菜或冷冻豌豆罐头上看不到骷髅图案，那么它们就一定是可以放心食用的，对吗？错！

尼克：好吧，我们在这里不要说得太过火了。我们这样说吧，罐头或冷冻食物不会要了你的命，但有更健康的吃法。问题是，很多人不再像你的奶奶一样有时间准备饭菜了。

苏珊：好吧，同意！但农民在他们的庄稼上喷农药，往他们的家畜里注射激素和抗生素，又怎么说？还可以放心食用这些肉吗？

尼克：这就是超市供应有机产品的原因。

苏珊：不要跟我提什么有机产品了！我们应该对那个产业中的很多东西持保留态度。

尼克：这个问题我们可以一直争论下去。你真的没得选择，除非你自己种蔬菜，自己养牲畜。但对于大部分人来说，那并不可行。

苏珊：这个话题我们各自保留意见吧，但有一点是可以肯定的，就是政府要介入。

跨文化交际小常识

　　在英美的社交场合中，女士往往被放在受人尊重的地位。男士处处都要谦让女士、爱护女士。步行时，男士应走在靠马路的一边，以免泥浆溅到女士身上；宴会上，当一位女士步入客厅时，厅里大多数男士都会站起来以表示尊敬；一位男士步入客厅，在场的女士不必起身；男女一起进入房间时，通常都是男士替女士开门；女士大多在男士之前走进房间或餐馆，除非男士走在前面替女士服务；用餐时，男士要帮助女士拉开椅子就座；在介绍时，人们通常把男士介绍给女士，除非男士社会地位很高或年岁很大。总之，男士在社交场合同女士接触时，一方面事事尊重她们，另一方面又要处处以保护人的姿态出现。

Section 3 Advanced 高级飞跃

万用表达一览

- [ ] **essential (to/for/that)** 极其重要的
- [ ] **value our health** 重视健康，把健康放在很重要的位置上
- [ ] **in tip-top shape** 最佳状态，巅峰状态
- [ ] **go on to** 接着（做另一件事），继续做，延续
- [ ] **join the workforce** 投身工作
- [ ] **Easier said than done!** 说起来容易做起来难！
- [ ] **look after our health** 关心 / 照料我们的健康
- [ ] **maintain a strict exercise regimen** 坚持严格的锻炼计划
- [ ] **well-balanced diet** 均衡的饮食习惯
- [ ] **It's best to start early.** 最好尽早开始。
- [ ] **ultimately, though** 虽然，最终
- [ ] **ensure a long and healthy life** 确保健康长寿
- [ ] **What do you think about that? /What do you have to say about that?** 你认为这些怎么样呢？ / 对这点，你怎么说？
- [ ] **follow** 按照
- [ ] **good guide to** 好向导，好指南
- [ ] **come to that realization** 意识到
- [ ] **by the time /by that time** 到那时，到那个阶段

万用表达详解

1. **essential (to/for/that)**

   释 very necessary (to do sth) 极其重要的

   例 It's essential to bide your time. "Haste makes waste", as they say.
   等待时机很重要，就像他们说的，"欲速则不达"。

127

2. **value our health**

    释 place value on one's health/take great care of 重视健康，把健康放在很重要的位置上

    例 As much as I value my health, I still can't be sure what's in the food I eat every day.

    尽管我非常注重健康，但还是无法确定自己每天吃的食物里含有什么成分。

3. **in tip-top shape**

    释 very fit/in great physical shape 最佳状态，巅峰状态

    例 I would say I'm in tip-top shape.

    我敢说我现在处于最佳状态。

4. **go on to**

    释 move on to 接着（做另一件事），继续做，延续

    例 After high school, I went on to university and studied for another six years.

    高中毕业后，我上了大学，又继续学习了6年。

5. **join the workforce**

    释 get a job/become a member of the employed 投身工作

    例 When I join the workforce in a few years, it's going to be very competitive.

    几年后我加入劳动大军时，竞争会更加激烈。

6. **Easier said than done!**

    释 Easy to say but difficult to do. 说起来容易做起来难！

    例 A: Have you ever tried skiing? Let me show you how it's done!

    你试过滑雪吗？我给你示范一下怎么滑吧！

    B: That's easier said than done. It's going to take me years to ski like you.

    这说起来容易做起来难。我得花上几年的时间，才能滑得像你那么好。

7. look after our health

释 take care of our health 关心 / 照料我们的健康

例 I must admit, I don't look after my health as well as I should.

我必须承认我对自己的健康没有给予应有的关心。

8. maintain a strict exercise regimen

释 follow a system of exercise 坚持严格的锻炼计划

例 My doctor told me to maintain a strict exercise regimen. If I don't, I won't get better.

医生告诉我说要坚持严格的锻炼计划，否则就不会痊愈。

9. well-balanced diet

释 eat all the right foods in moderation 均衡的饮食习惯

例 It's hard to maintain a balanced diet when you live away from home.

不在家住的时候，要保持均衡的饮食习惯很难。

10. It's best to start early.

释 The best way is to start early. 最好尽早开始。

例 If you want to learn English well, it's best to start early.

如果你想学好英语，最好尽早开始。

11. ultimately, though

释 but in the end 虽然，最终

例 I'd like to give you a job. Ultimately, though, I'm not the decision-maker.

我想给你一份工作，但我不是主事的人。

12. ensure a long and healthy life

释 guarantee a long and healthy life 确保健康长寿

例 A: How do you ensure a long and healthy life?

你怎么确保自己健康长寿呢?

B: I won't lie to you. I really don't know. Other than eating well, sleeping well and exercising regularly, I don't know what else you can do.

不骗你，我也不知道。除了吃好、睡好，定期锻炼，我也不知道你还能做些什么。

A: Maybe have the right genes!

或许还得有好基因！

B: Well done! I always knew you could do it.

太棒了！我就知道你能做到。

13. What do you think about that? /What do you have to say about that?

释 What do you think of that? 你认为这些怎么样呢？/ 对这点，你怎么说？

例 I just scored 100% on my English test. What do you have to say about that?

我英语考试得了满分，你认为怎么样？

14. follow

释 stick to/adhere to 按照

例 Follow the rules and you'll do just fine.

按照规则做，你就不会有问题了。

15. good guide to

释 instructions to 好向导，好指南

例 This is a good guide to Germany. Look, it even has a list of foods the Germans love to eat.

这是一本很好的德国指南。瞧，里面还有一张清单，列出了德国人爱吃的食物。

16. come to that realization

释 come to an awareness 意识到

例 I eventually came to that realization late in life.

终于，我在晚年意识到了这个问题。

17. by the time /by that time

释 expresses what has already happened at the time something else happens 到那时，到那个阶段

例 By the time the doctors diagnosed the problem, it was too late.

医生诊断出问题时，已经太晚了。

 实用对话场景

Susan: Our health is ***essential*** to live a normal life.

Nick: You're absolutely right! As we grow older we think about it more seriously.

Susan: Of course. We ***value our health,*** because it allows us to accomplish more. We need more energy for bigger tasks. School takes up a lot of time and energy. This is when we're at our peak.

Nick: So we need to be ***in tip-top shape***. But after we finish school and ***go on to*** university, or ***join the workforce***, our health becomes more important than ever.

Susan: ***Easier said than done!*** At home our parents remind us about ***looking after our health***, but after we leave home we have to get used to reminding ourselves.

Nick: Right. So, very often, people will join a sports club or gym and give themselves a ***strict exercise regimen***. Some people exercise better with others.

Susan: Diet is also critical as we get older. A ***well-balanced diet*** can be learned and maintained throughout one's life.

Nick: Yes. But ***it's best to start early.*** Fitness and diet require self-discipline.

Susan: That's right. But friends and family can be very helpful in reminding us to stay on track. ***Ultimately***, ***though***, it's up to us to maintain our bodies to **ensure a long and healthy life.**

Nick: Increasingly though, we're bombarded with many fad diets that often turn out to be harmful. **What do you think about that?**

Susan: The diet business is booming, because many people grow up without any real knowledge of what his or her body's needs are. Your biology textbook is enough to tell you which vitamins and minerals your body needs and which foods provide them.

Nick: **Following** your mother's recipes at home is also **a good guide to** healthy eating.

Susan: You hit the nail on the head! Learning basics like this from TV or magazines is often unnecessary and sometimes even foolish. People know that junk food is not healthy but insist on eating it.

Nick: Yeah. People often **come to that realization** late in life. **By that time** it's usually too late, and the damage has already been done.

Susan: Right. Heart disease, liver disease, diabetes, and obesity are just some of the avoidable, common diseases associated with poor diets that are plaguing the world today.

Nick: Too bad!

苏珊：身体健康对正常生活极其重要。

尼克：你说得对极了！随着年龄的增长，我们也更认真地对待身体健康。

苏珊：当然，我们重视身体健康，是因为它能让我们做更多的事情。我们需要更多的精力来完成更重要的任务。在校求学占用了我们大量的时间和精力，那是我们精力最旺盛的时候。

尼克：因此，我们需要保持最佳状态。当我们完成学业，继续上大学或投身工作时，身体健康变得比以往更加重要。

苏珊：说起来容易做起来难！在家里，父母会提醒我们关心健康，但离开家后，我们必须养成习惯，自己提醒自己。

尼克：没错。所以很多时候，人们会加入体育俱乐部或去健身房，给自己制订一个严格的锻炼计划。对有些人来说，与他人一起运动的效果更好。

苏珊：随着年龄的增长，饮食也变得很关键，我们要养成并一生坚持一个均衡的饮食习惯。

尼克：是的，但最好尽早开始。健身和饮食需要自制力。

苏珊：是的，但是朋友和家人的提醒对我们保持跟进也很有帮助，虽然最终还是要由我们自己来照顾自己的身体，以确保健康长寿。

尼克：但我们越来越多地被流行饮食轰炸，而这些最后常常被证明是有害的。你怎么看待这些呢？

苏珊：饮食业越来越兴隆，因为很多人在成长过程中并不真正了解他们的身体需要哪些营养。我们的生物教科书，就足以告诉我们身体需要哪些维生素和矿物质，哪些食物能够提供这些营养。

尼克：妈妈的家居食谱也是健康饮食的好向导。

苏珊：你说到点子上去了！没必要从电视或杂志上去了解这些基本的饮食习惯，有时那上面宣传的饮食习惯甚至是愚蠢的。大家都知道垃圾食品是不健康的，但还是一直在吃。

尼克：是啊！人们往往到了晚年才知道，但到那时，为时已晚，身体已经受到损害了。

苏珊：是啊！诸如心脏病、肝病、糖尿病及肥胖症这些可避免的、与不良饮食有关的常见疾病，困扰着整个世界。

尼克：太糟糕了！

跨文化交际小常识

"肢体语言"同常规语言一样，都属于文化的范畴。我们同别人谈话时，交际的手段不限于语句，我们的表情、手势和身体其他部位的动作，都向周围的人传递着信息。皱眉表示不满，挥手表示再见，这些动作都是交际手段的一部分。因此，要用英语进行有效的交际，在说话时就得了解对方的手势、动作、表情举止等这些肢体语言所表达的意思。如：食指与拇指构成圆圈，表示"OK"；伸开食指和中指表示"胜利"，耸动双肩表示"无可奈何"等。但由于中外很多肢体语言的含义存在着差别，因而对某种动作理解错了，也会自然而然引起一些意外的反应。如"跺脚"，汉语意义是气愤、灰心、悔恨；而英语意义表示为"不耐烦"。

读书笔记

Unit 11

Learning A Language
学习语言

万用表达一览

- ☐ **no environment to** 没有……的环境
- ☐ **I can only suggest...** 我只能建议……
- ☐ **meet up** 见面
- ☐ **a little weird** 有点奇怪
- ☐ **Have fun with it!** 享受其中的乐趣!
- ☐ **Not a bad idea!** 这主意不错!
- ☐ **I'll keep you posted!** 我会随时告诉你的!

万用表达详解

1. **no environment to**

   释 no ideal environment to (learn a language) 没有……的环境

   例 I want to learn English, but I have no environment to practice it in.

   我想学英语，但我没有练习的环境。

2. **I can only suggest...**

   释 My advice is... 我能只建议……

   例 I can only suggest you try the stores around the neighborhood.

   They might have what you're looking for.

   我只能建议你试试小区周围的商店，他们可能有你找的东西。

3. **meet up**

   释 get together with/meet 见面

例 A: Let's meet up after class.

我们下课后见面吧。

B: What time?

什么时候?

A: Say around 6?

大概 6 点?

B: You bet!

没问题!

4. a little weird

释 strange 有点奇怪

例 It feels a little weird coming back to this school after so many years.

这么多年以后重回这所学校，感觉有点怪。

5. Have fun with it!

释 Enjoy it! 享受其中的乐趣!

例 Here's a new game to learn English. Go ahead. Try it ! Have fun with it!

这是一个学习英语的新游戏，试试吧! 享受一下其中的乐趣!

6. Not a bad idea!

释 Good idea! 这主意不错!

例 A: You could say I went out of my way to speak English. I moved to the front of the bus this morning and just struck up a conversation with some native speakers on their way to work.

今天早上，我走到公交车的前排，跟一些在上班路上的、母语为英语的人搭讪。可以说，我是千方百计地练习英语啊。

B: Not a bad idea! Was it worth it?

不错的主意! 值得吗?

A: Definitely! They were all teachers and eager to help me.

当然！他们都是老师，都很热心地帮助我。

  B: That's the spirit!

  这样就对了！

7. I'll keep you posted!

  释 I'll keep you informed! 我会随时告诉你的！

  例 A: Any updates on the new schedule?

   新行程表里有什么更新吗？

   B: Nothing yet, but I'll keep you posted!

   还没有，但我会随时向您汇报的！

实用对话场景

May: I've just started learning English again. It's not easy. I have *no environment to* practice it in.

Ted: Yeah. I know what you mean. *I can only suggest* one thing to you.

May: What's that?

Ted: *Meet up* more often with people who speak better English than you do.

May: That's a great idea! I know a few friends of mine who use it every day. But it's *a little weird* using English with your friends.

Ted: Well, why don't you just joke around with English? *Have fun with it!*

May: *Not a bad idea!* I can do that. In fact that's a fantastic idea! I can't wait to try it out!

Ted: Well, I can't wait to hear the results.

May: *I'll keep you posted!*

梅：我已经重新开始学英语了，不容易啊，我没有练习的环境。

特德：是啊，我懂你的意思，我只能给你一个建议。

梅：什么建议？

特德：多跟英语说得比你好的人见见面。

梅：这主意真好！我认识几个朋友天天都说英语的，但跟朋友说英语有点怪。

特德：嗯，你为什么不用英语开开玩笑呢？享受这给你带来的乐趣嘛！

梅：这主意不错！我可以那样做。事实上那是个极好的主意！我迫不及待地想实践一下啊！

特德：嗯，我也迫不及待想知道结果。

梅：我会跟你保持联系的！

跨文化交际小常识

在英语国家，拜访某人需事先预约，忌突然造访。因突如其来的拜访会打乱他人的生活安排，给他们造成不便。在预约好后就要准时，不可提前或迟到。不过在赴宴时，美国人习惯晚5~10分钟，以便主人有足够时间换装接待，迟到超过20分钟以上最好电话告知原委，否则会被视为失礼的表现。如果有突发事件发生，无法前往，要提前通知，事后表达歉意，以弥补给主人造成的不便。在宴会、聚会或其他类似的社交活动中，英语国家的人们忌谈政事、公事或本行的事物，也最好避开涉及个人隐私的问题，如收入、宗教、婚姻状况等。聊天的话题最好是比较日常的而且是大家都比较熟悉的，如果你一人高谈阔论自己擅长的领域，也容易令人反感。

读书笔记

Section 2 ● Intermediate 中级进阶

万用表达一览

- [ ] **I feel like I'm hitting a brick wall.** 我感觉学不下去了。
- [ ] **keep bumping into** 老遇到
- [ ] **don't help much** 帮不了什么
- [ ] **I can't win!** （用愤怒的语气说）我真受不了了！
- [ ] **stuck in second gear** 没有完全发挥潜能
- [ ] **It beats me/God knows how!** 真打击我啊！问倒我了！真搞不懂！
- [ ] **a gift for** 对……有天赋

万用表达详解

1. **I feel like I'm hitting a brick wall.**

   释 I feel like what I'm trying to accomplish is hopeless. 我感觉学不下去了。

   例 A: Every time I try to learn this stuff, I feel like I'm hitting a brick wall.

   每次我学这东西，都感觉学不下去。

   B: Try a different approach.

   换个方法试试。

2. **keep bumping into**

   释 keep finding 老遇到

   例 I keep bumping into these knotty English phrases. I can't make head or tail of them.

   我老是碰到这些棘手的英语短语，我完全不懂。

3. **don't help much**

   释 are not very useful 帮不了什么

   例 Books like these don't help much if they don't give me

practical examples.

这样的书如果不给我实用的例子，就没什么用处。

4. I can't win!

释 Whatever I do, I can't get the upper hand (said in exasperation)（用愤怒的语气说）我真受不了了！

例 A: I just gave you the answer!

我刚刚回答过你了！

B: I know, but let me verify it online.

我知道，但让我上网核实一下。

A: Ah! I can't win!

唉！我真受不了了！

5. stuck in second gear

释 just existing/surviving without using one's full potential 没有完全发挥潜能

例 A: Do you ever feel like you're stuck in second gear?

你有没有曾经觉得自己没有完全发挥潜能?

B: Yeah. I just can't seem to catch a break!

是啊，我好像就是抓不住机会。

6. It beats me!/God knows how

释 I have no idea! /I'm baffled/perplexed! 真打击我啊！问倒我了！真搞不懂！

例 God knows how he does it! I'd have thrown it in the towel a long time ago.

天知道他是怎么做的！我早就已经放弃了。

7. a gift for

释 a talent for 对……有天赋

例 A: Some people definitely have a gift for languages, wouldn't you say?

一些人真的有语言天赋，你不觉得吗?

B: Yeah. I think you're probably right. But I also think that they probably organize themselves to learn languages better than the rest of us.

是啊，我觉得你可能是对的。但我也觉得他们很可能比我们其他人更有计划地学习语言。

 **实用对话场景**

May: I'm trying to learn more advanced English, but *I feel like I'm hitting a brick wall.*

Ted: Why? What's the problem?

May: I'm trying to follow the English in class, but *keep bumping into* these odd knotty phrases, weird sentence constructions and strange idioms. Dictionaries *don't help much*. Many online dictionaries have a lot of mistakes in both English and Chinese. *I can't win!*

Ted: What about your classmates?

May: My classmates seem to follow the native English lessons quite well, but I feel like I'm *stuck in second gear*. I want to learn more native English, but I have no real environment in which to learn it. *It beats me* how they do it! They must have *a gift for* languages or something.

Ted: Have you talked to your teachers about it?

May: A million times! But I get the same platitudes. "Try harder!" "Listen up in class!" "Contribute more in class!" "Get a summer job at Starbucks!"

Ted: Hey, that last one sounds interesting! Seriously, though, have you tried looking for native speakers to hang out with?

May: Yes. I do sometimes go out of my way to speak English, but it's not the kind of English that really helps me very much. There's only so much you can talk about with a stranger.

Ted: Welcome to the frustrations of learning a language. You know English has over a million words and countless expressions, idioms, proverbs, many of which, even native speakers never use. So don't beat yourself up too much about all the gaps in your English right now. Have you tried looking for a tutor?

May: Yeah. My mother signed me up a few times with different native speakers and I have made progress. I guess I just feel overwhelmed right now. I've got to get a handle on more advanced English or I'll never learn it.

Ted: You're not the first and certainly not the last to feel the pressure. Here's what I'd do if I were in your shoes. Go down to the new mall in town and look for some native books in that new bookstore there. Tell you what! I'll come with you. We'll pick up a few books that'll give you an edge. What do you say?

May: Thanks a million! I can't wait!

梅：我在试着学习更高级的英语，但我觉得学不下去了。

特德：为什么？有什么问题？

梅：在课堂上我试着去听懂英语，但我老碰到那些奇怪难懂的词组、奇怪的句子结构和习语。字典帮不了什么忙，很多在线词典有许多中英文解释错误。我不知道该怎么办了！

特德：那你们班同学呢？

梅：外教课我们同学好像上得相当不错，但我总觉得自己要差一些。我想多学一点地道的英语，但却没有真实的语境。我搞不清楚他们是怎么做的！他们肯定有语言天赋或什么。

特德：你跟你们老师说过这个问题没有？

梅：说过几万遍了！但我得到的都是陈词滥调："再接再厉！""在课上认真听讲！""在课上多发言！""在星巴克做暑期工！"

特德：嘿，最后一个建议听起来很有趣！但说正经的，你试过找一个以英语为母语的人来交往吗？

梅：嗯，有时我真的特意说英语，但那种英语对我真的没什么帮助。和一个陌生人聊天也只有那么多了。

特德：你现在感觉到学习语言带来的挫败感了吧。你知道英语有上百万个单词和无数的词句、习语、谚语，很多甚至连以英语为母语的人都没用过，所以不要因为现在英语上的不足而太责备自己。你找过家教没有？

梅：找过。我妈妈帮我找了好几个以英语为母语的外教，我也进步了。我想现在我只是有点不知所措而已，我要掌握更高级的英语，不然以后就学不成了。

特德：你不是第一个，当然也不会是最后一个感到压力的人。如果我是你，我会去闹市里的新购物中心，在那儿的新书店里找一些地道的英语书。告诉你吧，我会和你一起去，我们去买几本书，能让你比别人有优势的。你觉得如何？

梅：万分感激啊！我等不及了！

跨文化交际小常识

在英美国家，"请（Please）""对不起（Excuse me/Sorry）""谢谢（Thanks）"之类的词语随处可闻。无论是面对陌生人还是亲人，只要对方为自己做了点什么事，他们都会说声"谢谢"。在商店，收款员将零钱找回来时，他们会说声"谢谢"；学生回答完老师的问题后，老师也往往会表示感谢；餐馆里，服务员送上饮料和食物时，客人也会很客气地表示谢意。英美人还习惯于对别人说"对不起"。当一个人要从别人面前经过、向别人问路、中途离开、插话、提出异议时，他都要说声"对不起（Excuse me）"。在公共场所打嗝或与人交谈时打喷嚏、咳嗽都会被视为不雅，这时他都会说声"对不起（Sorry）"，表示歉意，请求对方原谅。

Section 3 Advanced 高级飞跃

万用表达一览

- [ ] **an opinion on the subject** 对某个话题的观点
- [ ] **it seems** 看来，似乎
- [ ] **come close to the mark/come close to** 接近目标，相当准确
- [ ] **fail dramatically/fail in dramatic fashion/fail spectacularly/fail miserably** 严重失败
- [ ] **learn by rote** 死记硬背
- [ ] **After all** 毕竟，终究，归根结底，别忘了（提醒某人时用）
- [ ] **Better yet** 更好的是，更妙的是
- [ ] **first things first** 最重要的事情应先做
- [ ] **as opposed to** 与……截然相反，反而
- [ ] **take the pain out of** 摆脱痛苦，变得容易
- [ ] **a real sense/a sense of** 一种……的感觉
- [ ] **at best** 最多，充其量
- [ ] **Be sure to...** 一定要，确保
- [ ] **at least** 至少
- [ ] **more of a reason** 更多的理由
- [ ] **put someone off** 使某人不感兴趣，（行为）使某人恶心

万用表达详解

1. **an opinion on the subject**

   释 a viewpoint on a matter 对某个话题的观点

   例 I was looking for help on a problem, but no one wanted to help me. So I solved the problem myself. Now everyone has an opinion on the subject.

   我当时在寻求帮助解决一个问题，但没人愿意帮我，所以我只

好自己解决了这个问题。现在每个人却对这评头论足。

2. **it seems**

释 it appears 看来，似乎

例 These days, it seems the world is upside-down.

如今，世界似乎颠倒了。

3. **come close to the mark/come close to**

释 come close to being accurate 接近目标，相当准确

例 Your definition comes very close to the mark, but it's still not quite right.

你的定义很接近了，只是还不完全正确。

4. **fail dramatically/fail in dramatic fashion/fail spectacularly/fail miserably**

释 completely fail 严重失败

例 He failed dramatically on his third attempt at the long jump.

在第三次试跳远时，他败得很惨。

5. **learn by rote**

释 learn by heart/memorize 死记硬背

例 I used to learn many things by rote. It didn't do me any harm. If anything, it gave me a great store of readily accessible knowledge.

我之前都是死记硬背，对我也没什么害处。相反，这种方法让我积累了很多有用的知识。

6. **After all**

释 In the end/After everything is said and done 毕竟，终究，归根结底，别忘了（提醒某人时用）

例 After all, as they say, "You can lead a horse to water, but you can't make him drink."

毕竟，正如人们所说的，"强扭的瓜不甜"。

7. **Better yet**

释 Even better 更好的是，更妙的是

例 A: We can drive there tomorrow and book a hotel room when we get there.

我们明天可以开车去那里，到了之后订个房间。

B: Better yet, we can book the hotel room now and save ourselves the trouble.

我们可以现在就预订房间，这样比较好，也可以省去一些麻烦。

8. **first things first**

释 the most important things first 最重要的事情应先做

例 A: I need to discuss something with you. It's rather important.

我需要和你讨论一些非常重要的事情。

B: First things first. Have you had breakfast? Do you want to grab a coffee?

最重要的事情应先做。你吃过早餐了吗？你想喝杯咖啡吗？

A: You're right. Let's grab something to eat. I'd rather not talk about this with an empty stomach.

你说得对，我们先买点东西吃吧，我可不愿空着肚子跟你谈论这件事。

9. **as opposed to**

释 in contrast to 与……截然相反，反而

例 It's better in the long run to be more agreeable, as opposed to argumentative, if you want to get ahead in life.

如果想要在生活中取得成功，从长远来看，还是随和点好，不要那么好争辩。

10. **take the pain out of**

释 make it easier and less stressful 摆脱痛苦，变得容易

例 You know what they say, "Many hands make light work." Working together takes the pain and frustrations out of the job.

你知道有句话是这么说的："人多好办事。"团队合作可以减轻工作带来的痛苦和沮丧。

11. a real sense/a sense of

释 a feeling of 一种……的感觉

例 I'm getting a sense of déjà vu in this place, as if I've been here before.

我对这个地方有种似曾相识的感觉，好像我之前来过这儿。

12. at best

释 (not a real complement.) the best I can say is... 最多，充其量

例 A: What do you think of the new maid?

你觉得这个新来的佣人怎么样啊?

B: At best, she's helpful in the kitchen. Even then she needs a lot of supervision.

她最多也就能在厨房里帮点忙。即使那样，也需要时时有人监督。

13. Be sure to...

释 Make sure to 一定要，确保

例 Be sure to tell me when you're leaving.

你走的时候，一定要告诉我。

14. at least

释 good thing/at the minimum 至少

例 A: Are you OK? I see you have a few scratches on your face.

你还好吧? 我看到你脸上有几处擦伤。

B: I'm OK. At least I wasn't the one driving. I'd be in real trouble right now if I had been.

我还好，至少我不是开车的人，不然我就真的很惨了。

15. more of a reason

释 a stronger reason to do 更多的理由

例 A: I need more of a reason than that to help you.

我需要比那更有力的理由才帮你。

B: What more reason do you need?

你需要什么更充足的理由呢？

A: A good enough reason. Say, diligence. Would you call yourself diligent?

一个合理的理由，比如说，勤奋。你会说自己勤奋吗？

B: Absolutely. All the more reason to help me then, right?

当然。那就有充分的理由帮我了，对吧？

A: Give me one good reason why I should trust you.

给我一个充分的理由让我相信你。

B: We've been friends for a long time. Isn't that reason enough?

我们做朋友很久了，这个理由还不够吗？

A: All right you've twisted my arm.

好吧，你赢了。

16. put someone off

释 make someone sick to their stomach/repel/repulse sb. 使某人不感兴趣，（行为）使某人恶心

例 You really know how to put someone off with your attitude.

你的态度真让人恶心啊。

实用对话场景

May: How do you learn a language anyway?

Ted: Learning a language is easier said than done.

May: Everyone has *an opinion on the subject*. Every day, *it seems*, some new book or video claims to teach a language faster and easier than before.

Ted: Some claims *come close to the mark*, though. Others *fail dramatically.* All I can say is that *learning* vocabulary *by rote* isn't enough. ***After all,*** you don't speak like that, do you? You speak in coherent sentences. That's exactly the way you should learn whatever language you're learning.

May: But I don't use many of the phrases I learn off by heart.

Ted: No problem. Learn them in context. Learn them as part of a topic. ***Better yet***, learn them in the form of a dialogue. Pay attention to your pronunciation. Look for the opportunity to use what you've learned soon after memorizing the phrases. That'll help solidify the new words and phrases in your mind.

May: Someone also advised me to learn the formal versions of the same phrases.

Ted: Yes, but ***first things first***. Learning what you need to say first, ***as opposed to*** what you want to say, will ***take the pain out of*** learning a language, and give you ***a real sense*** of accomplishment at the same time.

May: That's really good advice.

Ted: I don't claim to have all the answers when it comes to learning a language. I just know from my own experience. Learning vocabulary by rote didn't help me, because I didn't know how to put the words together. Plus, I didn't know the most suitable phrases to express what I wanted to say. ***At best***, learning words by rote can help your comprehension and allow you to speak somewhat coherently.

May: What you're really saying is, it can allow you to speak a 'broken' English, for example. But it must sound strange to anyone listening to it.

Ted: Yes. You could put it like that. Learning phrases as part of a simulated dialogue can be very helpful. In no time you can have real conversations.

May: Let's not forget idioms.

Ted: Right. Idioms are useful. **Be sure to** practice your accent too, so that the words, phrases or idioms you use will **at least** give the listener **more of a reason** to talk to you. Your accent and voice, along with your use of vocabulary and phrases can definitely attract or **put** someone **off**. Good luck with your language studies.

May: Thanks.

梅：你是如何学习一门语言的？

特德：学习一门语言说起来容易做起来难。

梅：关于这个话题，每个人都有自己的观点。似乎每天我们都可以看到一些新的书籍、新的视频，声称能够使你比以前更快更轻松地掌握语言。

特德：有些确实有效，但有些根本不理想。我只能说，用死记硬背的方式学习词汇是不够的，毕竟我们不会那样说话，不是吗？我们是用连贯的句子说话的，而这正是学习任何一门语言都应该采用的方法。

梅：但我很少用硬背下来的短语。

特德：没关系。你可以联系上下文、把它们当成话题的一部分去学习，更好的方法是用对话的方式学习，并注意你的发音。尽快找机会运用你所学过的语句，这样才能帮助你巩固这些新单词和语句。

梅：有人也建议我要学习这些词句的书面体。

特德：是的，但是最重要的事要放在首位。相对于你所希望说的东西而言，首先要学习你所需要说的，这样才能使你摆脱学习过程中的痛苦，从而得到真正的成就感。

梅：这真是很好的建议。

特德：我并不是说在语言学习方面，我都有方法，这些只是从我个人的经验中总结出来的。词汇学习上，死记硬背对我并没有帮助，因为我不知道怎么将这些词汇贯穿起来。另外，我也不知道什么词最适合用来表达我想说的话。死记硬背单词顶多能让你理解词汇，说一些蹩脚的英语罢了。

梅：你其实是想说，背诵词汇只能让你说一些"不连贯"的英语，这肯定听起来很怪吧。

特德：是的，你可以这么说。模拟对话的方式对学习短语有很大的帮助，不用多久你就能够用英语进行真实的对话了。

梅：不要忘了还有俚语。

特德：对，俚语很有用。还有一定要注意口音，这样你使用那些词汇、短语或者俚语时，才至少能让听者更愿意与你交谈。你的口音和声音，还有你所使用的短语和词汇，绝对可以吸引或吓跑听众。愿你在学习语言中一帆风顺。

梅：多谢！

跨文化交际小常识

英美人，尤其是美国人，喜欢别人直呼自己的名字（given name/first name）。与人交往之初，可以用"姓氏（family name/last name）"称呼对方，但稍微熟识之后便可直呼其名。可以直呼Jack、John，但不能将Jack和John与 Mr/Miss/Mrs/Ms 连用；可以说Mr/Miss/Mrs/Ms Green，但不能说Mr Jack。在英美国家，很少有人称呼别人的头衔，除非是称呼那些从事特定工作的人，如法官、医务工作者、博士、教授、政府高级官员、宗教领袖等，而这些头衔往往放在姓氏的前面。例如：Senator Green（格林参议员）；Dr. Bethune（白求恩大夫）。但值得注意的是，英美人从来不用局长、经理、主任、校长等官衔称呼别人。

Unit 12

Plants
植物

万用表达一览

☐ **need a hand** 需要帮忙

☐ **a long way off from** 很长时间以后

☐ **Unlike us** 不像我们

万用表达详解

1. **need a hand**

   释 need some help 需要帮忙

   例 A: Do you need a hand?

   　　你需要帮忙吗?

   　　B: No, I'm fine, thanks.

   　　不用，我可以的，谢谢。

2. **a long way off from**

   释 not in the near future/far from/a long way away from 很长时间以后

   例 A: Do you think we'll see meteor showers like the ones in that movie *2012*?

   　　你觉得我们会看到像电影《2012》里那样的流星雨吗?

   　　B: I think we're a long way off from that.

   　　我觉得我们还要等很长时间呢。

   　　A: Well, I'm not so sure about that.

呃，我不敢苟同。

3. Unlike us

释 not like us 不像我们

例 Unlike us, our parents already have it made.

不像我们，我们的父母已经成功了。

实用对话场景

John: Are you going to the garden nursery today?

Selina: Yeah. I'm going to pick up some daffodil bulbs for the garden.

John: Daffodil bulbs? Isn't it a little cold for daffodils right now?

Selina: No. It's spring. It's the best time for them.

John: OK. Hey, do you ***need a hand*** trimming the trees?

Selina: No. We're ***a long way off from*** that. Fall is the best time for trimming. We don't want to hurt the trees.

John: Wait a minute. Trees can feel?

Selina: Sure. Just like any creature. You just don't hear them say "Ouch!" But trees can also heal themselves and regenerate their limbs.

John: ***Unlike us.***

Selina: Do you want to give me a hand planting the daffodils now?

John: You bet!

约翰：今天你打算去苗圃场吗？

赛琳娜：是啊，我打算买些水仙花球装饰花园。

约翰：水仙花球茎？现在种水仙花不是有点冷吗？

赛琳娜：不，现在是春天，是种水仙花的最佳时节。

约翰：好吧。嘿，你需要帮忙修剪树木吗？

赛琳娜：不，我们很久之后才修剪呢，秋天才是修剪的最佳季节，我们不想对树木造成伤害。

约翰：等一等，树能感觉吗？

赛琳娜：当然，就像所有的生物一样，你只是没听见它说"噢"而已。
　　　　但树也可以自愈，然后重新长出枝节。

约翰：不像我们。

赛琳娜：现在你想帮我种水仙花吗？

约翰：当然！

跨文化交际小常识

　　在国际商务活动中，中西方文化之间存在个人本位的竞争观与群体本位的和谐观的差异：西方从事商务工作的人员具有很强的个人奋斗意识和竞争意识，强调个人的作用，通常个人也有足够的权力来处理各类日常和突发事务。企业鼓励雇员个人奋斗，不断创新，个人能力是以个人的实际经营业绩为基础，将个人能力与企业报酬和补偿结合为一体。而中国的企业文化往往更加强调个人利益服从群体利益，企业利益服从国家利益。个人的成就由企业和国家共同分享。个人的成就不是看他个人的能力如何出众，而是看个人为企业和国家的公众福利事业做出了多少贡献。和谐作为一个极具深刻历史传统的文化价值观念，在企业的经营活动中表现为公平、均富和稳定。

读书笔记

Section 2　Intermediate 中级进阶

万用表达一览

☐ **in particular/particularly** 特别是

☐ **first off** 首先

☐ **No wonder...** 怪不得……

☐ **Not nearly enough!** 这样做还远远不够！／远不止这些呢！

☐ **affect** 影响

☐ **act as/like** 表现得像

☐ **Here's the real kicker!** 这才是你意想不到的呢！／这个才是重点！

☐ **Where do you get this stuff?** 你在哪儿找到／学到这个东西的？

☐ **How about that!** 真没想到啊！

万用表达详解

1. **in particular/particularly**

   释 specifically 特别是

   例 I don't like his manner, particularly the way he tries to dominate a conversation.

   我不喜欢他的行为举止，特别是他试着主导对话的方式。

2. **first off**

   释 first of all 首先

   例 First off, let me just say that I'm really grateful to everyone for their help.

   首先这样说吧，我真的很感谢他们的帮助。

3. **No wonder...**

   释 It's no surprise that... 怪不得……

   例 A: You're the spitting image of that actor on those TV commercials.

No wonder people keep staring at you.

你跟那些电视广告里的那个演员真的很像，怪不得大家老盯着你看。

B: I had no idea.

我之前不知道呢。

4. Not nearly enough!

释 far too little 这样做还远远不够！/ 远不止这些呢！

例 A: Governments around the world are trying to stem overfishing in their waters.

世界各国政府都在尝试遏止在他们水域里的过度捕捞行为。

B: Not nearly enough!

这样做还远远不够！

5. affect

释 influence/work on 影响

例 A: How do you think his poor grades are affecting him?

你觉得他成绩不好对他有什么样的影响？

B: I think he's pretty down about them.

我觉得他很沮丧。

6. act as/like

释 behave like 表现得像

例 He acts like he's all that.

他表现得就像自己很特别一样。

7. Here's the real kicker!

释 Here's the most surprising part (of the story)! 这才是你意想不到的呢！/ 这个才是重点！

例 A: That restaurant has been charging customers based on their nationality! They just figure that some nationals spend more than others.

那间餐馆一直根据顾客的国籍收费！他们认为一些国家的顾

客比其他人花更多的钱。

B: That's disgraceful!

那样做很不光彩!

A: And here's the real kicker! They got caught red-handed and were hit with a hefty fine!

最让人惊讶的是，他们被当场抓捕了，而且还被重罚呢!

B: Serves them right!

他们罪有应得!

8. Where do you get this stuff?

释 Where do you find out/learn about these things? 你在哪儿找到 / 学到这个东西的?

例 A: Where do you get this stuff?

你怎么发现这个的?

B: I read very selectively.

我是有选择地阅读的。

9. How about that!

释 Very interesting! That's surprising! 真没想到啊!

例 A: Scientist just discovered another earth-like planet in our galaxy.

科学家刚刚发现了我们星系里的另一颗类地行星。

B: Well, how about that!

真想不到啊!

实用对话场景

John: We were discussing plants in class today, trees *in particular*. Really fascinating stuff!

Selina: In what way?

John: Well, *first off*, trees are enormously beneficial to the environment. They suck up the carbon monoxide and carbon dioxide from the air and give off oxygen.

Selina: *No wonder* we see so many trees along highways.

John: *Not nearly enough!* But another thing they do is to cool the air, especially in summer. Have you ever noticed how cool it is under a tree? Now imagine millions upon millions of trees cooling the air. That can really *affect* the temperature around us.

Selina: So they *act as* air-conditioners too. What else?

John: Well, trees are also habitats for creatures from birds to caterpillars to bacteria. They all have a valuable part to play in our ecosystem. And *here's the real kicker!*

Selina: What's that?

John: Bacteria, like the "pseudomonas syringae" found in trees, help make rain and snow. In fact, just one of these might make enough protein molecules for a thousand snow crystals.

Selina: *Where do you get this stuff?*

John: In school.

Selina: *How about that!*

约翰：今天我们在课上讨论植物，特别讨论了树木。树木真的是很有趣的东西！

赛琳娜：在哪些方面有趣？

约翰：首先，树木对我们的环境有极大的好处，它们吸收空气中的一氧化碳和二氧化碳，并释放出氧气。

赛琳娜：怪不得我们看到高速公路边上有那么多树了。

约翰：远不止这些呢！树木的另一个作用是冷却空气，特别是在夏天。你以前留意过在树下有多凉快吗？现在想象一下，几百万棵树一起冷却空气，那真的能影响我们周围的气温。

赛琳娜：所以树木也有空调的作用。还有呢？

约翰：嗯，树木还能给大至鸟类小至毛虫、细菌等生物提供栖息地，它们在我们的生态系统中都扮演着重要的角色。下面才是你想不到的呢!

赛琳娜:是什么?

约翰:在树上发现的像假单胞菌这样的细菌有助于雨雪的形成。事实上,只要其中一个细菌就可能有足够的蛋白质分子来形成一千多朵雪花了。

赛琳娜:你从哪儿学来的?

约翰:在学校。

赛琳娜:真想不到啊!

跨文化交际小常识

和中国人相仿,在西方也忌讳生病和死亡的话题。他们常常用pass away、fall asleep来代替die(死亡),用big C代替cancer(癌症)。即便本人生病了,也不直说I am ill而代之I don't feel well。体态语是话语的重要组成部分,也是不同文化习得的结果。西方人交谈时喜欢有适当的目光接触,以示对谈话的重视和交谈人的真诚,但中国人感觉直视对方很不礼貌;和美国人谈话,发现他们在强调自己的观点和争辩时,常用食指指着对方,这使中国人也很不舒服,觉着尊严有所冒犯;而中国人在说错话或者尴尬时,下意识会伸伸舌头,尤其女孩还喜欢捂着嘴笑,英美人士会认为他们受到了轻视和侮辱。

读书笔记

Section 3 Advanced 高级飞跃

万用表达一览

☐ **Not just that!** 不只是那些。

☐ **would look a lot like** 看起来会更像，更类似于

☐ **much of** 大部分

☐ **Speaking of** 说到（起）

☐ **covered in** 覆盖于，淹没在

☐ **Why is that?** 怎么会那样？

☐ **source of** ……的来源

☐ **serve other functions** 有其他功能

☐ **serve as habitats** 作为动物、昆虫等的栖息地

☐ **as you well know** 如你熟知，如你所知

万用表达详解

1. **Not just that!**

   释 Not only that. 不只是那些。

   例 A: He's leaving tomorrow.

      他明天走。

      B: Not just that! He's leaving for good!

      岂止这样！他是要永远离开！

2. **would look a lot like**

   释 closely resemble 看起来会更像，更类似于

   例 Guangdong without its heavy rainfall would look a lot like Inner Mongolia.

   要是没有充足的降水量，广东看起来就会很像内蒙古了。

3. **much of**

   释 a lot of 大部分

例 Much of the region was devastated after the earthquake.

地震后，这个地区的很多地方都毁了。

4. **Speaking of**

释 Talking of 说到（起）

例 Speaking of games, what did you have in mind?

说到游戏，你心里有何想法？

5. **covered in**

释 sth. was all over him/her/it 覆盖于，淹没在

例 He walked into the room covered in sawdust.

他走进一间到处都是锯末的房间。

6. **Why is that?**

释 Why? 怎么会那样？

例 A: We can't get a lift to the next village.

我们不能搭顺风车到下一个村庄去了。

B: Why is that?

怎么会那样？

A: Because people here don't pick up hitchhikers like we do back home.

因为这里不像我们国家，人们是不会搭乘过路人的。

7. **source of**

释 where something originates ……的来源

例 These kinds of stories were a source of great amusement long ago, before TV and movies.

这种故事在很久之前，还没有电视和电影的时候，是一种很好的娱乐方式。

8. **serve other functions**

释 have other uses 有其他功能

例 These cable cars have served other functions in the past. They weren't always used to ferry tourists between mountain peaks.

这些缆车在过去还有其他的功能，他们不只是用来在山峰之间运送游客的。

9. serve as habitats

释 act as shelter/places for animals/insects etc

作为动物、昆虫等的栖息地

例 Trees serve as habitats for a variety of species, including birds and insects.

树木是包括鸟类和昆虫等许多物种的栖息地。

10. as you well know

释 You know this very well 如你熟知，如你所知

例 As you well know, I'll be retiring next year.

你也很清楚的，我明年就退休了。

实用对话场景

John: Plants are essential to our world. They provide the nourishment, including the necessary vitamins and minerals, which we need to maintain a healthy life.

Selina: **Not just that!** Plants provide shade against the scorching sun. Without plants our planet **would look a lot like** the Sahara Desert. Plants also supply us and other life-forms with oxygen and consume **much of** the CO_2 we produce.

John: Of course plants exist on land and in water.

Selina: **Speaking of** water, 70% of the earth is **covered in** water.

John: Oceans would not be able to support life without the vital work of plants.

Selina: **Why is that?**

John: Well, plants are **a source of** nutrition, shade, oxygen, not to mention minerals, such as Nitrogen(N), Phosphorus (P),

Potassium(K), Calcium(Ca), Magnesium(Mg) and Sulfur(S).

Selina: Plants, such as trees, ***serve other functions*** as well. They're not just a source of timber and shade for us humans, but also ***serve as habitats*** for animals like birds and monkeys.

John: Let's not forget that plants also serve as habitats for insects and bacteria, which, ***as you well know***, is essential to our planet's ecosystems.

Selina: This has really been interesting. I look forward to our next chat.

约翰：植物对我们的世界来说是必不可少的。它们提供人体所需的营养物质，包括我们所需的维生素和矿物质，以使我们保持健康的生活。

赛琳娜：不只是这些。在烈日下，植物能够遮阴。没有植物，我们的地球看起来会更像撒哈拉沙漠。此外，植物还为我们和其他生命体提供氧气，并吸收我们产生的二氧化碳（CO_2）。

约翰：当然，植物生长在陆地上和水里。

赛琳娜：说起水，地球表面的 70% 被水覆盖着。

约翰：没有植物的重要作用，海洋将无法维持生命体。

赛琳娜：那是为什么？

约翰：嗯，植物是营养、树荫、氧气的来源，更不用说它们也是各类矿物质的来源了，比如氮（N）、磷（P）、钾（K）、钙（Ca）、镁（Mg）以及硫（S）。

赛琳娜：像树木这样的植物还有其他功能。它们不仅为我们人类遮阴、提供木材，也是鸟类、猴子等动物的栖息处。

约翰：不要忘了，植物也是昆虫、细菌等的栖息地。正如你所知，它们对我们地球的生态系统是极其重要的。

赛琳娜：这真的很有趣，我期待着下次聊天。

跨文化交际小常识

中国人旅游的基本模式是：上车睡觉，下车撒尿，景点拍照。这本也无可厚非，但倘若不注意有些地区，尤其境外地区，有些民族对于拍照的禁忌，就难免身处尴尬，甚至面临罚款或法律指控。看见可爱的外国小宝宝长得如天使般可爱，忍不住就想拍下来，但在澳洲，未经父母允许，擅自给未满14岁的儿童拍照是违法的，更别提将其放到朋友圈、INS、Facebook等社交媒体上了。泰国是"千佛之国"，但在参观寺庙时，忌讳给佛像和僧侣拍照。阿联酋禁止对政府机构、王宫和外国驻阿领事馆建筑拍照，违反者将受严厉处罚。在希腊也禁止游客对一些古迹进行拍照。在美国一些博物馆如纽约的大都会，华盛顿D.C.的航空航天博物馆、艺术博物馆等地方也是禁止拍照的，必须自觉遵守当地的拍照规矩。还有大多数国家和地区的海关及机场禁区都禁止拍照，拿出手机都要被工作人员阻止。涉及宗教、文物和私人的地方，一般拍照都会遭到限制。

读书笔记

Unit 13

What Should I Do? I
我该怎么办？（一）

万用表达一览

- [ ] **What's troubling you?** 什么事困扰着你啊？
- [ ] **handle it myself** 自己搞定
- [ ] **blow off some steam** 发泄一下
- [ ] **talk it over** 倾诉出来
- [ ] **One thing that's bothering me** 困扰我的一件事是……
- [ ] **giving me a hard time** 总让我难堪
- [ ] **speak up in class** 课堂上发言
- [ ] **bound for** 向往，飞往
- [ ] **Judging by** 从……上看（判断）
- [ ] **Chances are...** 有可能……

万用表达详解

1. **What's troubling you?**

   释 What's the matter?/What's bothering you? 什么事困扰着你啊？

   例 A: What's troubling you?

   　　什么事困扰着你啊？

   B: My entire stamp collection went up in smoke yesterday.

   　　我收集到的邮票昨天全化为灰烬了。

2. **handle it myself**

   释 take care of it/manage it myself 自己搞定

例 Don't worry about helping me with the essay. I can handle it myself.

不用担心要帮我写论文，我自己可以搞定。

3. blow off some steam

释 release some pent-up anger 发泄一下

例 I got into an argument with them today. I guess I just needed to blow off some steam.

今天我和他们吵架了，我想我只是要发泄一下而已。

4. talk it over

释 discuss a matter/problem/issue 倾诉出来

例 A: If you want to talk things over, my door is always open.

如果你想把事情说出来，我的大门随时为你打开。

B: Thanks.

谢谢！

5. One thing that's bothering me...

释 One matter that is troubling me is... 困扰我的一件事是……

例 One thing that's really bothering me is his manner. He's always making snide remarks about me.

惹我生气的是他的言行举止，他总是对我冷嘲热讽。

6. giving me a hard time

释 making life difficult for me 总让我难堪

例 Some of my classmates are giving me a hard time.

我的一些同学总让我难堪。

7. speak up in class

释 Make oneself heard in class/Voice one's opinion 课堂上发言

例 I try to speak up in class more often now.

现在我试着在课堂上多发言。

8. bound for

释 headed for 向往，飞往

例 Some of my classmates are bound for foreign universities, some of which are quite prestigious.

我的一些同学准备上国外的大学，其中有一些大学相当有声望。

9. **Judging by**

释 based on 从……上看（判断）

例 Judging by the handwriting, this must be yours.

从字迹上判断，这肯定是你的。

10. **Chances are**

释 There is a likelihood 有可能

例 Chances are, we'll meet up again next year.

我们明年有可能会再见面。

实用对话场景

Bob: So **what's troubling you?**

Tina: It's OK. I can **handle it myself** . But thanks!

Bob: Well, if you need to **blow off some steam** or **talk it over**, let me know.

Tina: Well, there is **one thing that's bothering me**.

Bob: What's that?

Tina: Some of the guys in school were **giving me a hard time** because I always **speak up in class**. They call me names.

Bob: Yeah, well, just ignore them. Let me guess. These guys aren't **bound for** top schools like you, are they?

Tina: **Judging by** their grades, they're not!

Bob: Well then, what are you worried about? **Chances are**, you won't be seeing them again next year.

鲍勃：你有什么烦心事儿吗？

蒂娜：没事，我自己可以处理。但还是谢谢你！

鲍勃：嗯，如果你需要发泄或倾诉，告诉我。

蒂娜：嗯，有件事真的很困扰我。

鲍勃：是什么事儿？

蒂娜：因为我老在课堂上发言，学校里有些男孩儿总让我很难堪，他们给我起绰号。

鲍勃：是吗，那就别搭理他们。让我想想，这些家伙应该不像你那样想去顶尖的学校，对吗？

蒂娜：从他们的成绩来看，是的！

鲍勃：那你还担心什么？下学期你就不会再见到他们了。

跨文化交际小常识

　　世界上每个国家或民族都有共同的节日，如中国的春节、西方的圣诞节、伊斯兰教的古尔邦节等，人们在过节时都怀着美好的愿望，希望冲走晦气，来年好运，所以在过节时会对自己的某些行为加以约束，一些节日禁忌也由此而生。圣诞节是西方最盛大的节日，它的禁忌主要和圣诞布丁有联系。西方人在做圣诞布丁时，每个成员都至少来搅动一下，并许下心愿，且要注意往顺时针方向搅动，心愿也不要向任何人透露，据说这样才达成所愿。元旦是中西方人共同庆祝的节日，英美人十分重视这一天的来临，对这天的言行举止也格外重视。他们相信元旦的第一位访客是怎样的人将决定这一年的运势，所以他们会有意做些安排，有幸被邀请的第一位访客可以做几户人家甚至整一条街的首位拜访者。被邀请者应在新年钟声敲响之后及时登门，以防不祥之人捷足先登。

读书笔记

Section 2 Intermediate 中级进阶

万用表达一览

☐ **Can't complain!** 还过得去！马马虎虎！

☐ **Could be worse!** 不算很糟！（情况糟，但不算最糟，可能会更糟）

☐ **settling in** 安居，适应

☐ **still adjusting** 还在适应

☐ **There you go!** 就这样了！

☐ **make the transition** 调整

☐ **So far, so good.** 目前为止一切都好！

☐ **Not soon enough!** （对我来说）也没有很快啦！

万用表达详解

1. **Can't complain!**

   释 Things are fine/OK. 还过得去！马马虎虎！

   例 A: How's life in Guangzhou?

   　　广州的生活怎样？

   　　B: Can't complain!

   　　还过得去！

2. **Could be worse!**

   释 Things are not good but could be worse. 不算很糟！（情况糟，但不算最糟，可能会更糟）

   例 A: How's your new neighborhood?

   　　你新的邻居怎样？

   　　B: Could be worse!

   　　还可以吧！

3. **settling in**

   释 getting comfortable 安居，适应

例 I'm just settling in here for the time being. It's nothing permanent!

我只是暂时在这里住一住，不是永久居住的！

4. **still adjusting**

释 still adapting to (my new surroundings/environment) 还在适应

例 I'm still adjusting to my new schedule.

我还在适应我的新行程表。

5. **There you go!**

释 That's the way it is! 就这样了！

例 I've spoken to him about it, but he doesn't want to listen. So there you go. I've done what I can. The ball's in his court now!

我已经告诉过他了，但他不愿听，所以就这样了。能做的我都做了，现在那是他的事了！

6. **make the transition**

释 make the change 调整

例 I need to make the transition quickly or I'll be left behind.

我要快点调整，不然我就要落后了。

7. **So far, so good.**

释 Up until now things are fine. 目前为止一切都好！

例 A: My essay needs just one more paragraph.

我的论文还有一段就写好了。

B: Great! So far, so good!

太棒了！目前为止一切都好！

8. **Not soon enough!**

释 Not fast enough for me! （对我来说）也没有很快啦！

例 A: The summer holidays are almost here!

暑假快到了！

B: Not soon enough!

也没有很快啦！

实用对话场景

Bob: So how are things in school?

Tina: **Can't complain!** How about you?

Bob: **Could be worse!**

Tina: So you're not **settling in** very well then. Is that it?

Bob: Yeah, well, it's a new school. I'm **still adjusting**. I miss my old school, but **there you go.** What can you do? I have to adapt to it.

Tina: Yeah. Same here. I switched schools last year and had to **make the transition. So far, so good.**

Bob: Glad to hear it.

Tina: Don't worry. The year is almost over.

Bob: **Not soon enough!**

Tina: I hear you!

鲍勃：在学校过得如何？

蒂娜：还过得去！你呢？

鲍勃：不算很糟！

蒂娜：这么说你并不是很适应，对吧？

鲍勃：对，这是我的新学校嘛，我还在适应中。我想念我以前的学校，但就这样了。你还能怎样？我得适应。

蒂娜：是啊，我也是。去年我转学了，不得不调整自己。目前为止一切尚好。

鲍勃：很高兴听到你这样说。

蒂娜：别担心，今年快结束了。

鲍勃：也没有很快啦！

蒂娜：我懂！

跨文化交际小常识

中国文化关注过去和现在，较少注重未来；美国文化则很少关注过去，主要着眼现在和未来。在以过去为导向的文化中，过去的经历和发生的事件是最重要的，所以人们要尊重传统和祖宗传下来的智慧。在解决现实问题时，在历史的长河中寻找"药方"总是正确的。在以将来为导向的文化相信明天或将来的某一时间是最重要的，目前所从事的工作不是为了履行而履行，而是为了将来潜在的利益。欧美有许多国家便属于这种重视将来的文化。时间价值取向的不同反映在商务活动中，美国人更讲究计划性，时间观念很强，视时间为有限的资源。

读书笔记

Section 3 Advanced 高级飞跃

万用表达一览

☐ **have some issues to work through** 有些问题要解决

☐ **get some pointers** 得到一些指点

☐ **I'll give it a shot** 我会试一试

☐ **So, let me get this straight.** 让我来理理思路，我来给你理一理，那我就直说了。（多用于批评某人时）

☐ **grades are slipping** 成绩下滑

☐ **let things get to you** 让事情 / 问题影响你

☐ **Does that about sum it up?** 概括起来是那样吗？

☐ **falling out** 闹翻，吵架

☐ **cut ties with** 远离某人，少来往

☐ **drop them** 与他们断绝来往

☐ **surround yourself** 让你的周围拥有

☐ **reach my goals** 实现我的目标

☐ **set unrealistic goals** 制订不切实际的目标

☐ **set short-term realistic goals** 设定短期而又现实的目标

☐ **little by little** 逐渐地，一点点地

☐ **judge the results** 评价成果，判断结果

☐ **adjust your goals** 调整你的目标

☐ **treat me like a child** 把我当成小孩子看待，像小孩子一样对待我

☐ **Look!** 听我说！

☐ **go through a phase** 正经历着人生的一个阶段

☐ **What do I do?/What do I do about it?** 我该怎么办呢？ 我要做什么呢？

☐ **That's a tough one!** 这挺难的！

☐ **taking your studies more seriously** 更加认真地对待你的学习

☐ **stay out of trouble** 少惹麻烦事

☐ **let little things derail your life** 让一点点的小事打乱你的生活

☐ **not as bad as all that** 没那么糟，没那么严重

☐ **it feels that way** 确实感觉如此

☐ **The bottom line is** 归根结底是，底线是

☐ **Don't sweat the small stuff...** 不要为小事烦恼不已

☐ **grow up** 长大

☐ **If only my parents saw it that way.** 如果我父母那样认为就好了。

万用表达详解

1. **have some issues to work through**

   释 have to solve some personal problems 有些问题要解决

   例 I need to work through some issues. It'll take some time.
   我有些问题要解决，得花点时间。

2. **get some pointers**

   释 get some advice 得到一些指点

   例 Let me give you a few pointers before you start.
   在你开始之前，我得给你做些指点。

3. **I'll give it a shot**

   释 I'll try it 我会试一试

   例 I've never done this before, but I'll give it a shot.
   这个我之前从没做过，但我会试一试的。

4. **So, let me get this straight.**

   释 Let me understand this correctly. (often used before telling someone off) 让我来理理思路，我来给你理一理，那我就直说了。（多用于批评某人时）

   例 A: I really need a hand with English before the test tomorrow.
   我的确需要有人在明天考试前帮我补习一下英语。

B: So, let me get this straight. You slept through English classes all the term, and now you're worried about your English test tomorrow?

那我就直说了！这个学期的英语课，你都在睡觉，现在你才担心明天的英语考试吗？

5. grades are slipping

释 grades are falling/getting worse 成绩下滑

例 A: All work and no play makes Mike a dull boy.

只用功不玩耍，聪明的孩子也变傻。（只工作不休息，人会变呆的。）

B: What am I supposed to do? My grades are slipping, and I've been grounded for a month.

我该怎么办呢？我的成绩一直下滑，都被禁足一个月了。

6. let things get to you

释 let problems affect you 让事情／问题影响你

例 A: Why don't you want to go to school?

你为什么不想上学？

B: I'm having a little trouble in school.

我在学校惹了点麻烦。

A: You can't let these things get to you. Missing school will only make things worse.

你不能让这些事情影响你，逃课只会让事情变得更糟。

7. Does that about sum it up?

释 Is that a good enough summary of the issue? 概括起来是那样吗？

例 A: You spent last month goofing off and now you're anxious about your exams. Does that about sum it up?

上个月你都在混日子，现在你才担心考试，我概括得对不对啊？

B: That's about it.

差不多吧。

8. **falling out**

释 argument followed by a period of little or no communication 闹翻，吵架

例 A: Why don't you invite Sarah along to your birthday bash?

你为什么不邀请萨拉来参加你的生日聚会呢？

B: Actually, we've had a falling out. We haven't spoken (to each other) in a while.

实际上，我们闹翻了，我们有段日子没说话了。

9. **cut ties with**

释 stop communicating with sb. 远离某人，少来往

例 I suggest you cut ties with them. They're going to hurt your image.

我劝你不要跟这些人来往，他们有损你的形象。

10. **drop them**

释 cut ties with them 与他们断绝来往

例 If your so-called "friends" are interfering with your long-term ambitions, you should drop them.

如果你所谓的朋友阻碍了你长远的目标，你就应该跟他们断绝来往。

11. **surround yourself**

释 keep/have (certain types of people) around you 让你的周围拥有

例 You should surround yourself with nicer friends.

你应该交一些好点的朋友。

12. **reach my goals**

释 fulfill my aim/objective 实现我的目标

例 It'll take me some time to reach my goals.

要实现目标，还需要一段时间。

13. set unrealistic goals

释 set unattainable aims 制订不切实际的目标

例 You should never set unrealistic goals for yourself. You'll only be disappointed in the end.

你不应该给自己制订不切实际的目标，最后你只会失望。

14. set short-term realistic goals

释 Plan to fulfill achievable aims over short periods of time. 设定短期而又现实的目标

例 It's best to set short-term realistic goal.

最好是设定短期而又现实的目标。

15. little by little

释 bit by bit 逐渐地，一点点地

例 Little by little we're getting a handle on things.

我们会慢慢明白这些事情的。

16. judge the results

释 评价成果，判断结果

例 I think it's too early to judge the results.

我认为现在判断结果，还为时过早。

17. adjust your goals

释 change your goals 调整你的目标

例 It's probably wise to adjust your goals every so often.

偶尔调整一下自己的目标应该是很明智的做法。

18. treat me like a child

释 talk down to someone as if they were a child 把我当成小孩子看待，像小孩子一样对待我

例 I'm sick and tired of being treated like a child. I'm 16 now. Enough already!

我受够了，不愿再被当作小孩来看待。我已经 16 岁了，够了！

19. Look!

释 Listen to me! 听我说！

例 Look! I'm very sorry for the way I spoke to you. That was uncalled for.

听我说！我对自己和你说话的方式表示歉意，那样做是不应该的。

20. go through a phase

释 go through a difficult maturing period in someone's life 正经历着人生的一个阶段

例 A: She's so unpredictable. One day she's happy. The next day she's moody.

她太喜怒无常了，一会儿高高兴兴的，一会儿又闷闷不乐的。

B: She's just going through a phase. Don't worry about it.

她只是正经历着人生的一个阶段，不用担心。

21. What do I do?/What do I do about it?

释 What can I do?/What plan of action can I take?/What course of action can I take? 我该怎么办呢？我要做什么呢？

例 My parents are getting on my back about my grades. What do I do about it?

我父母总是唠叨我的成绩，我该怎么办呢？

22. That's a tough one!

释 That's a difficult problem! /That's a tough nut to crack! 这挺难的！

例 A: I'm fat. I need to lose weight. What can I do about it?

我太胖了，我要减肥。我该怎么做呢？

B: That's a tough one. Exercise as much as possible but keep eating well. That should do the trick.

这挺难的。尽量锻炼，正常饮食应该有用。

23. taking your studies more seriously

释 be serious/focused on your studies 更加认真地对待你的学习

例 A: My parents keep telling me to take my studies more seriously.

我父母一直告诉我要更加认真地对待学习。

B: They want what's best for you. That's all. My parents also harped on me for years. Look where I am now.

他们是望子成龙啊。我父母也这样跟我唠叨了好多年，看看我现在怎么样了。

24. stay out of trouble

释 Don't get into trouble. 少惹麻烦事

例 A: Be sure to stay out of trouble. It's easy to get caught up in that element.

别惹麻烦，不然很容易就会和那帮不三不四的人搅在一起的。

B: What element?

什么不三不四的人？

A: You know perfectly well. The guys you've been hanging out with. They're bad news!

你很清楚，就是整天和你混在一起的那帮人，他们都是惹是生非的人！

25. let little things derail your life

释 give a chance to little things to disturb your life 让一点点的小事打乱你的生活

例 Why do you let these little things derail your life?

为什么让这些小事打乱你的生活呢？

26. not as bad as all that

释 not all that bad 没那么糟，没那么严重

例 Stop whining about that. It's not as bad as all that. It could be worse.

不要再抱怨了，没那么严重，抱怨只会让事情变得更糟。

27. it feels that way

释 You feel that way 确实感觉如此

例 A: It's not all that bad.

没那么糟。

B: Well, it feels that way.

嗯，确实如此。

28. The bottom line is

释 Most important is this/The most important concern is this/The overriding concern is this 归根结底是，底线是

例 The bottom line is, I can't afford to go. It's as simple as that.

归根结底，我没有足够的钱去那儿，就这么简单。

29. Don't sweat the small stuff...

释 Don't worry about minor issues! 不要为小事烦恼不已

例 My teacher keeps saying things like, "Don't sweat the small stuff" but I always do.

我们老师经常说："不要钻牛角尖"，但我老是那样。

30. grow up

释 mature 长大

例 At some point, we all have to just grow up and stand on our own two feet.

从某一角度来说，我们都要长大，并要自食其力。

31. If only my parents saw it that way.

释 I wish my parents would think of it like that. 如果我父母那样认为就好了。

例 If only you could see it that way.

如果你那样认为就好了。

实用对话场景

Bob: I can't really speak for you or tell you what to do. You obviously **have some issues to work through** on your own.

Tina: It would really help me to **get some pointers** from you.

Bob: OK. **I'll give it a shot**! **So, let me get this straight.** You're having trouble in school. Your **grades are slipping**, and you're **letting things get to you**. **Does that about sum it up**?

Tina: Yeah. Just about.

Bob: OK. Let's start with the **falling out** you had with your classmate. He's a bad influence on you. It's a difficult decision to **cut ties with** people, but if they're unhealthy to be around, **drop them**. **Surround yourself** with people who lead healthy, well-adjusted lives.

Tina: Another thing. I can't seem to **reach my goals.**

Bob: Maybe you **set unrealistic goals** for yourself. Try **setting short-term realistic goals**, so that **little by little** you'll be able to **judge the results** earlier and **adjust your goals** as needed.

Tina: I have another question for you. I'm almost an adult, but my parents **treat me like a child.**

Bob: **Look!** You're **going through a phase**. You want your independence, but you're dependent on your parents.

Tina: So, **what do I do?**

Bob: **That's a tough one.** I'd say, show your parents that you're more mature by **taking your studies more seriously** and **staying out of trouble**. If you are, as you say, "more of an adult now", then they'll see that and give you more freedom. But if you **let little things derail your life**, then you are still very immature and need to be guided. It's **not as bad as all that.** But at your age **it feels that way.**

Tina: So, **the bottom line is**: I should surround myself with people who lead healthy and well-adjusted lives, set short, realistic goals for myself but adjust them when necessary, and most importantly **not sweat the small stuff** if I want others to take me seriously.

Bob: I think you've **grown up** a lot in the last few minutes.

Tina: Now **if only my parents saw it that way.**

Bob: They will. Give them some time.

鲍勃：我真的不能替你说什么，也不能告诉你该做什么。很显然，有些问题要你自己去解决的。

蒂娜：要是你能给我一些指点，那我会受益匪浅的。

鲍勃：好吧，试试吧，那我就直说了。你在学校里遇到了麻烦，你的成绩也在不断地下滑，这些让你感到心烦意乱。大概是这样，对吧？

蒂娜：是啊！就是这样的。

鲍勃：好吧，我们先来谈谈你和同学闹翻的事情吧。对你，他产生了坏的影响。与人绝交的确是个非常困难的决定，但是如果他们在你周围产生了不良影响，你就应该和他们断绝来往，并且应当与那些有着健康的生活方式且适应力强的同学为伴。

蒂娜：还有，我似乎很难实现自己的目标。

鲍勃：也许是因为你为自己制订的目标不太切合实际。你可以试着为自己制订切实可行的短期目标。这样，你就可以早点一步步地评价你的成果，并按需要调整自己的目标了。

蒂娜：我还有一个问题想问你，我都已经差不多是成年人了，但我父母依然把我当成小孩看待。

鲍勃：好好听着！你正在经历人生中的一个阶段，你渴望独立，而事实上你还在依赖你的父母。

蒂娜：所以，我该怎么办呢？

鲍勃：这个问题挺难的。我觉得，你可以通过更加认真地学习和不闯祸来证明给你的父母看，你变得更成熟了。如果你真的已经变得如你所说的"更像大人了"，那你的父母一定能够体会到，并给你更多自由。但是，如果一点点的小事就能打乱你的生活，那么你仍然是不成熟的，依然需要父母的监督指导。实际情况并没那么糟，但在你的这个年纪，情况看起来又确实如此。

蒂娜：所以，要点是：尽可能地与生活作风良好的人为伍，为自己设立切合实际的短期目标，并在必要时对其进行适当调整。最重要的是，如果你想让别人认真对待你，就不要为一点儿小事烦恼不已。

鲍勃：在刚才的几分钟，我觉得你已经长大了许多。

蒂娜：要是我父母这样认为就好了。

鲍勃：他们会的，给他们一些时间吧。

跨文化交际小常识

美国人对山楂花与玫瑰花非常偏爱。在动物之中，美国人普遍爱狗。美国人认为：狗是人类最忠实的朋友。对于那些自称爱吃狗肉的人，美国人是非常厌恶的。在美国人眼里，驴代表坚强，象代表稳重，它们分别是共和党、民主党的标志。美国人最喜爱的色彩是白色。在他们看来，白色象征着纯洁。除此之外，人们还喜欢蓝色和黄色。由于黑色在美国主要用于丧葬活动，因此，美国人对它比较忌讳。美国人最讨厌的数字是"13"和"3"。他们不喜欢的日期则是星期五。相传，耶稣的门徒犹大，为了贪图三十枚银币而出卖了耶稣，并使耶稣惨死在十字架上。在意大利著名画家达·芬奇的名画《最后的晚餐》中描绘耶稣被出卖前和门徒共进晚餐，其中第十三个人就是叛徒犹大。耶稣遇难的那天正好是"星期五"。故此，西方人把"13""星期五"视为凶险的数字。同时，美国人和西方人还忌讳"3"。据说，在第一次世界大战中，有一天晚上，有不少士兵因抽烟暴露目标而被击毙，其中因点第三支烟而死的居多。因此，西方人有"一火不点三支烟"的习俗。

Unit 14

What Should I Do?
II 我该怎么办？（二）

万用表达一览

- [ ] **cram for** 突击复习，刻苦学习，过分用功，苦读
- [ ] **to come up for air** 休息一下
- [ ] **drop everything** 放下所有的一切
- [ ] **get out for a breather** 出去透透气，出去透透风
- [ ] **first things first** 先处理要事
- [ ] **score well on** 在……上得到好成绩
- [ ] **That's key right now.** 那是目前要紧的事！
- [ ] **hit the books** 用功读书

万用表达详解

1. **cram for**

    释 swot/study excessively 突击复习，刻苦学习，过分用功，苦读

    例 A: How about a game of badminton later?

    　　晚点打羽毛球怎么样？

    B: Sorry, I really need to cram for my finals, so I'm going to have to drop badminton for now.

    　　不好意思，我真的要为期末考临时抱佛脚了，所以我要暂时放一放羽毛球了。

2. **to come up for air**

    释 to take a break 休息一下

例 You've been hitting the books hard this week. You need to come up for air sometime.

这个星期你学习很用功，需要找个时间休息一下。

3. **drop everything**

释 stop doing something immediately (to do sth. else) 放下所有的一切

例 A: Are you moving overseas?

你要移民吗？

B: No. I can't just drop everything here and see how it goes. I need to plan ahead.

不，我不能放下这里的一切，看一步走一步，我需要先规划好未来。

4. **get out for a breather**

释 go outside for some fresh air 出去透透气，出去透透风

例 A: What do you say we walk the dog?

我们去遛狗怎么样？

B: Good idea! I really need to go out for a breather.

好主意！我真的需要出去透透气。

5. **first things first**

释 do not try to do things in the wrong order, omitting an important basic step 先处理要事

例 A: First things first! How did the test go?

先说正事！考得怎么样？

B: Better than expected, but not as well as I had hoped!

比预期的好，但没有我期望的好！

6. **score well on**

释 get a good grade on 在……上得到好成绩

例 I scored well in math but low in English.

我数学分数高，但英语分数低。

7. That's key right now.

释 That's essential right now. 那是目前要紧的事！

例 A: What are you up to these days?

这段时间你在忙什么？

B: Organizing myself for the finals. That's key right now!

准备考试。那是眼下最要紧的事！

8. hit the books

释 study one's books very hard/well 用功读书

例 I need to hit the books really hard over the holidays, so I'll be ready for my summer exams.

假期我真的要好好"啃书"，这样的话我就能准备好这个夏季考试了。

实用对话场景

Sally: So what's it like in school these days?

Paul: What do you think?

Sally: A rat race?

Paul: Yeah，especially this year. Everybody's **cramming for** their finals. I just can't get a minute to relax.

Sally: Well, you need **to come up for air** sometimes. Do you have any time for sport?

Paul: I really had to **drop everything** for the finals. My parents were dead set against me playing on weekends. But I need to **get out for a breather** once in a while.

Sally: Yeah. Absolutely! Right now, though, **first things first. Score well on** your finals. **That's key right now.**

Paul: How do you deal with the pressure?

Sally: It's no difference for me. I have to **hit the books** like everyone else.

Paul: Well，fingers crossed we both do well!

Sally: Yeah. Fingers crossed!

萨莉：现在学校怎么样？

保罗：你觉得呢？

萨莉：竞争激烈？

保罗：对，特别是今年。期末考大家都拼命啃书，我一分钟都没休息过。

萨莉：嗯，有时你需要透透气。你有时间做运动吗？

保罗：为了期末考我真的不得不抛下一切。我父母坚决反对我周末玩，但我需要偶尔出去透透气。

萨莉：是啊，当然要！但现在要先解决头等大事，现在关键是期末考高分。

保罗：你怎么排解这些压力？

萨莉：我也没什么不同，也得像其他人一样啃书。

保罗：嗯，祝咱俩都考个好成绩！

萨莉：好，祝我们好运！

跨文化交际小常识

　　在英美国家，人们在邮局、银行等公共场合办事时，在餐馆用餐或加油站加油时，都严格按照先来后到的顺序排队，并保持一定的距离，他人不得加塞儿。不得不近距离通过他人时，以"excuse me"（打扰了）告知下。在公共场合与他人交谈时，注意控制音量，禁止大声喧哗。在上下楼梯、搭手扶梯或者走路时，都要注意站在左边，将右边空出来以便对面行人通过，即所谓出行"左立右行"。打喷嚏或咳嗽时，要用纸或手绢捂着鼻子，转过身去，绝对不能冲着他人打喷嚏，事后别忘了说：excuse me（对不起），周围的人也会报以善意地说：God bless you（上帝保佑你），以此祝福你消灾祛病，身体安康。

Section 2 　Intermediate 中级进阶

万用表达一览

- [ ] **what I should do with my life** 我这辈子 / 我的人生该做些什么（通常表达"该选择怎样的人生职业""该实现怎样的人生目的"）
- [ ] **Don't rule it out.** 不排除这种可能性。
- [ ] **have to say about** 对……怎么说
- [ ] **play to my strengths** 发挥所长
- [ ] **make a living** 谋生
- [ ] **have a solid profession** 拥有一份固定的工作
- [ ] **fall back on** 依靠
- [ ] **be around the block** 经验丰富
- [ ] **improve on** 改进，使更好

万用表达详解

1. **what I should do with my life**

   释 usually expresses what career to choose for life/what purpose one's life should serve 我这辈子 / 我的人生该做些什么（通常表达"该选择怎样的人生职业""该实现怎样的人生目的"）

   例 I can't tell you what you should do with your life. That's your decision. I can only offer you a few suggestions. Reading biographies can also give you some pointers.
   我无法告诉你该过怎样的人生，那要你自己来决定。我只能给你一些建议，读传记也能给你一些启发。

2. **Don't rule it out.**

   释 Don't dismiss the possibility of something/Don't believe something can't happen/exist 不排除这种可能性。

例 A: I don't think there will be any math quiz this week.

我觉得这周没有数学小测。

B: Don't rule it out. Our math teacher is full of surprises these days.

不要排除这个可能性，我们数学老师这段时间可是常有意外惊喜哦。

3. **have to say about**

释 have an opinion on 对……怎么说

例 A: What does that book have to say about future careers?

关于未来职业生涯，那本书上怎么说？

B: It says that we should all aim to be as talented as possible in different areas.

里面说，我们都应该尽可能培养自己的才华。

4. **play to my strengths**

释 do what comes naturally/what one is good at 发挥所长

例 She always encourages them to play to their strengths.

她总是鼓励他们发挥所长。

5. **make a living**

释 earn money/work 谋生

例 I will need to make a living once I graduate from university.

我大学毕业后就要立刻谋生了。

6. **have a solid profession**

释 have a profession that earns well/brings in a steady income

拥有一份固定的工作

例 I want a solid profession after I graduate from university.

我想在毕业之后有一份固定的工作。

7. **fall back on**

释 have in reserve in case of an emergency 依靠

例 Make sure you have something solid to fall back on.

你一定要有份可以依靠的稳定的工作。

8. be around the block

释 had plenty of experience (good and bad) 经验丰富

例 He's the best person to give you advice. He's been around the block. He knows what he's talking about.

他是能给你建议的最佳人选，他见多识广，知道自己在说什么。

9. improve on

释 make better 改进，使更好

例 I can't improve on that. It's perfect just the way as it is.

那个我不能再改进了，这样就已经很完美了。

实用对话场景

Sally: I need to know **what I should do with my life.**

Paul: Well，what are you good at?

Sally: Well, I'm good at the clarinet, but I don't think I'll be playing for an orchestra.

Paul: **Don't rule it out**. What else are you good at?

Sally: I like drawing, and my teacher often tells me that I'm a natural.

Paul: So you're artistic. That's for sure! What about the sciences? Do you have a head for math?

Sally: Not my strong suit, I have to say.

Paul: What do your parents **have to say about** it?

Sally: They tell me to **play to my strengths**, but to make sure I can **make a living** from it. If not, at least **have a solid profession** to **fall back on**.

Paul: I have to say, they're right. They've **been around the block**, you know. Here's what I think you should do. Try to **improve on** your weaknesses. Who knows, you may develop other strengths. Math is extremely important, so don't neglect it.

Learn a profession that's related to one of your interests but also financially rewarding.

Sally: Thanks for the tip.

Paul: Anytime.

萨莉：我要知道这辈子该做些什么。

保罗：嗯，你擅长什么？

萨莉：我擅长单簧管，但我觉得我不会为一个管弦乐队演奏。

保罗：不要排除这种可能。你还擅长什么？

萨莉：我喜欢画画，我的老师常常说，我是个有天赋的人。

萨莉：这么说你肯定很有艺术才华！理科方面呢，你在数学方面能力强吗？

保罗：我得说，这不是我的强项。

萨莉：你父母怎么说？

保罗：他们告诉我，要发挥所长，但这个"长处"必须是我可以维持生计的。如果不是，至少要有一份固定的可以依靠的工作。

萨莉：我必须说，他们是对的。你知道，他们经验丰富。我觉得你应该试着改进你的弱点。谁知道呢，你也许会发展出其他强项呢。数学是尤其重要的，所以不要忽视它。学一技之长，既与你的兴趣相关，又在经济上有回报的。

保罗：谢谢你的建议。

萨莉：不用谢。

跨文化交际小常识

在交际场合，美国人喜欢主动跟别人打招呼，并且乐于主动找人攀谈。如果乐意，美国人是可以跟任何人交上朋友的。美国人的见面礼节，大约是世界上最简单不过的。在一般情况下，同外人见面时，美国人往往以点头微笑为礼，或者只是和对方"嗨"一下作罢。不是特别正式的场合，美国人甚至连国际上最为通行的握手礼也略去不用了。若非亲朋好友，美国人一般不会主动与对方亲吻、拥抱。美国人的处世风格，总体上是潇洒浪漫。他们主张充分地享受生活，凡事都要尽可能地去尝试下。在平时，他们喜欢笑面人生，爱开玩笑。跟美国人相处时，若是不明白这点，而是一味地恪守"喜怒不形于色"的中国古训，无形中会使对方与自己拉开距离，甚至让对方对自己敬而远之。

读书笔记

Section 3 ● Advanced 高级飞跃

万用表达一览

☐ **Live life to the max** 全身心地投入生活，活得充实

☐ **have an ace up your sleeve/have a fallback** 运筹帷幄，胸有成竹，有后备计划，有锦囊妙计，有王牌

☐ **have it all** 拥有想要的一切

☐ **breeze through life** 顺利地通过，轻松地取得成功

☐ **land on one's feet** 化险为夷，安然脱险

☐ **learn some basic life skills early on/learn some fundamentals early on** 早早学会了一些基本的生存技能

☐ **what sets some people apart from others** 让一些人从社会/经济/智慧方面有别于其他人的东西

☐ **I get you.** 我理解你。

☐ **resilient** 适应力强的，从不幸中能够迅速恢复的

☐ **face setbacks** 面对挫折

☐ **couldn't write to save their lives** 文章写得很糟糕／很烂

☐ **in the blink of an eye** 一眨眼工夫

☐ **weigh up choices** 权衡选择

☐ **All good things come with setbacks.** 好事多磨。

☐ **Don't paper over mistakes.** 不要掩饰错误，纸包不住火。

万用表达详解

1. **Live life to the max**

   释 Live life to the full 全身心地投入生活，活得充实

   例 A: Many people these days want to live life to the max.
   现在很多人都想全身心地投入生活。

B: What does that really mean?

那其实意味着什么呢？

A: It means getting the most potential from your life.

意味着最大限度地发挥生命的潜质。

B: That makes sense.

有道理。

2. **have an ace up your sleeve/have a fallback**

释 have a back-up plan 运筹帷幄，胸有成竹，有后备计划，有锦囊妙计，有王牌

例 In case things don't work out as expected, I always have an ace up my sleeve.

以防事与愿违，我通常都会有后备计划。

3. **have it all**

释 have everything you want 拥有想要的一切

例 A: Some people want to have it all.

有些人什么都想要。

B: I know what you mean. They want to have their cake and eat it too.

我明白你的意思，他们想鱼和熊掌兼得。

4. **breeze through life**

释 go through life without a care 顺利地通过，轻松地取得成功

例 I certainly didn't breeze through life. I worked hard for everything.

我当然不是轻而易举就成功的，每件事我都很努力去做。

5. **land on one's feet**

释 succeed no matter what the obstacles 化险为夷，安然脱险

例 I always seem to land on my feet. Don't ask me how I do it. I just do.

我好像总能化险为夷，别问我是怎么做到的，我就是做到了。

6. **some fundamentals early on**

释 learn essential skills at an early age 早早学会了一些基本的生存技能

例 All highly successful people seem to have one thing in common. They've all learned some basic life skills early on in life.

所有非常成功的人都有一个共同点，那就是他们在人生的早些时候就已经学会了一些基本的生存技能。

7. **what sets some people apart from others**

释 something distinguished people socially/economically/intellectually etc./something makes some people special 让一些人从社会／经济／智慧方面有别于其他人的东西

例 I guess it's those little things that set us apart.

我认为是那些小细节把我们和其他人区分开来的。

8. **I get you.**

释 I understand you. 我理解你。

例 I think I get you. You're saying it's better to focus on my studies now and put other things aside until later.

我想我明白你的意思。你是说现在最好把精力放在学习上，其他事先放一放。

9. **resilient**

释 able to pick oneself after a fall/able to start all over again 适应力强的，从不幸中能够迅速恢复的

例 She's very resilient. Even this minor setback won't stop her from winning.

她心态很好，这点小挫折是阻止不了她获胜的。

10. **face setbacks**

释 deal with reversals of fortune 面对挫折

例 We all face setbacks from time to time.

我们都有遇到挫折的时候。

11. couldn't write to save their lives

释 hopeless at something 文章写得很糟糕 / 很烂

例 One thing I'll say about him is this: He's very smart, but he couldn't write to save his life.

关于他，我要说的一点是，他很聪明，但文章写得很烂。

12. in the blink of an eye

释 very quickly 一眨眼工夫

例 She lost millions of dollars in the blink of an eye.

一眨眼的工夫，她就损失了数百万美元。

13. weigh up choices

释 consider the choices 权衡选择

例 I need to weigh up my choices very carefully before I decide.

在做出决定之前，我需要仔细权衡各个选择。

14. All good things come with setbacks.

释 All successes come with reversals of fortune. 好事多磨。

例 I guess it's true what they say, "All good things come with setbacks".

我认为他们说的是真的，"好事多磨"。

15. Don't paper over mistakes.

释 Don't try to hide mistakes/Don't cover up mistakes. 不要掩饰错误，纸包不住火。

例 I was always taught never to paper over mistakes. If I made a mistake, I'd admit to it and deal with it, even if I were punished for it.

别人老教育我不要掩饰错误。如果犯了错，我必须承认并着手解决，即使我会因此而受到处分。

 实用对话场景

Sally: What can I tell you? **Live life to the max.** Study hard, so that you'll always **have an ace up your sleeve**.

Paul: But some people seem to **have it all.**

Sally: Some people are lucky and seem to **breeze through life.** They always seem to **land on their feet,** never seem to work very hard, and have what they all want. But that's not quite true.

Paul: What do you mean?

Sally: I mean, they've learned some basic life skills early in life. That's **what sets some people apart from others**: learning to do what's necessary first.

Paul: I think **I get you**. People, who have mastered certain concepts early in life, tend to be more **resilient** and better prepared to **face setbacks**.

Sally: Exactly. Just ask the high-school drop-out-turned millionaire, whose best subject may have been math. I've known successful people who **couldn't write to save their lives**, but when it mattered, they could turn a cool million **in the blink of an eye.**

Paul: I've heard stories like that.

Sally: So you ask me what you should do with your life. The short answer is to do what you enjoy, but that's not always the best answer.

Paul: What would you suggest then?

Sally: I would suggest that you take care of fundamentals first. Be able to take care of yourself physically and mentally. Learn math. It's essential for a productive life. Learn early to **weigh up choices** properly. If something is too good to be true, it usually is. **All good things come with setbacks.** So learn to take the good with the bad in everything, without giving up on your long-term goals.

Paul: I still don't have any long-term goals.

Sally: Well, whatever long-term goals you decide on, make sure that your quality of life improves and doesn't deteriorate. Don't do anything in haste. You'll just end up spending more time or money fixing the problems later. ***Don't paper over mistakes.*** Correct them early. In a nutshell, live like you have one chance to get things right. That way, even if you do make mistakes, they are fruitful lessons and not bitter memories.

Paul: That's really great advice. Thanks a million.

Sally: Anytime.

萨莉：我该怎么跟你说呢？全身心地投入到生活当中，并努力学习，这样你就能够一直保持优势了。

保罗：但有些人似乎拥有一切。

萨莉：有些人很幸运，而且看起来很轻松地就能取得成功，不管发生什么他们总是能够化险为夷，似乎永远不用努力工作，却总能得到自己想要的东西。其实不然。

保罗：你的意思是？

萨莉：我是说，他们早已经学过一些基本的生存技巧了。首先学做必要的事情，这能让一些人优于其他人。

保罗：我想我明白你的意思了。谁先掌握了某些理念，谁就会有更强的适应能力，能够更好地面对挫折。

萨莉：完全正确。问问那些高中就辍学而成为百万富翁的人吧，他们最好的学科可能是数学。我认识一些成功人士，文章写得很糟糕，但在关键时刻，他们可以瞬间赚取百万。

保罗：我听说过那样的故事。

萨莉：所以，你问我你应该怎样生活，简单的回答就是做你喜欢的事情，但这并不总是最好的回答。

保罗：那你有什么建议？

萨莉：我会建议你首先打好基础，有能力处理好自己身心两方面的事情。学习数学，这对于一个富有成效的生活是很重要的。早点学会如何做出正确的选择。如果一件事情好得让人难以置信，那么事实大抵如此。好事多磨嘛，所以学会接受生活中的好与坏，不要放弃你的长期目标。

保罗：我还没有长期目标呢。

萨莉：不论你的长期目标是什么，要确保你的生活品质是在不断提高而不是在下降。不要草率地做任何事情，否则，最终你将会花更多的时间和金钱来解决日后出现的问题。不要掩饰错误，应尽早予以纠正。总的来说，人生就是把握好机会。这样一来，即使你犯了错误，也是宝贵的经验教训，而不是痛苦的回忆。

保罗：真是不错的建议，非常感谢！

萨莉：不客气。

跨文化交际小常识

　　中国人偏爱偶数，但忌讳4，因为和"死"谐音，我们偏好8和6，也是谐音"发"和"顺"的缘故，所以宴请宾客用6个菜或8个菜招待，包压岁钱也是666元或888元，讨个好彩头。而西方人畏惧13和5的数字。通常建筑大楼的楼房和房间没有13层和13号房间，学生不安排13号考场，请客时也避免13人一桌。对这些数字的忌讳来源于圣经的故事。传说耶稣和他的十二门徒共进最后的晚餐时，第十三个人正是犹大，他为了30个银币，将耶稣出卖，耶稣被钉死在十字架的日期也是13号（星期五）；而人类的祖先亚当和夏娃偷食禁果被逐出伊甸园的日子也恰巧是13号（星期五）。所以，在西方人的观念里，星期五同样不吉利，他们称之为Black Friday（黑色星期五），A Friday moon brings foul weather（星期五的月亮会带来坏天气）的习语也体现了西方人对星期五的厌恶。

读书笔记